TRANSFORMING
G.R.O.W.T.H.

TRANSFORMING
G.R.O.W.T.H.

God's Design for Personal and Church Growth

Dan Stanley, Ph.D.

TRANSFORMING **G.R.O.W.T.H.**

© 2018 by Dan Stanley, Ph.D.

Printed in the United States of America

ISBN: 978-0-578-41286-3
   1. Nonfiction—Church Growth. 2. Nonfiction—Christian Life—Spiritual Growth.

www.InternationalGrowthInstitute.com
Cover design by Shawn Morgan
Interior Layout by Hailey Radabaugh

CONTENTS

ACKNOWLEDGMENTS

Jesus is the Alpha and Omega, the Beginning and End, the First and the Last, and therefore gains any credit for this faith-work endeavor. I want to thank Him for the life He has given me to share with my incredible wife and co-laborer, Jan. She is the exceptional grace I have been given to help me heal and grow in my spiritual journey. Jan has given me three awesome children who have given us many grandchildren that bring us joy and youthfulness. My wife is the strength I need in my life to help encourage me to do it God's way and get His results. She is the most important person in my life. I would also like to thank the people, staff, and leaders of RockFish Church that have given me the privilege to serve alongside them for nearly a quarter of a century making the Name of Jesus Spectacular. My life was sent on a trajectory into ministry by four special men and their families for which I am grateful; Fidel Jimenez, Joe Rodrigues, Michael Fletcher, and my brother Chuck Stanley. They all had given me the very important gift of having faith in my life when I did not; for this, I am appreciative beyond words. I would also like to thank my best friend and accountability partner, Mark McVickers. Mark, along with his wife, Annie, and family, have helped me in ways too numerous to acknowledge in this short space. Two of my closest friends and co-workers in the faith, Darren and Claudia Clark have made my journey successful in a multitude of ways. The Associate Pastors of RockFish, Tony McVickers, Nathan Stanley (my son), and Youth Leader, Dustin Wittington have helped carry the load of the ministries with endless commitment. Alan Keen, the Worship Director, is my good friend that has brought passion to corporate worship at RockFish. For all of them, and many others I give my thanks; they are all special God-given gifts.

1

INTRODUCTION

The lack of vitality seen in the Church today drives home the need for God-given design protocols. Violation of these protocols has led to a depletion of disciples that are free from psychological, physiological, emotional, and spiritual sickness. In a recent American Cultural and Family Institute survey, conducted February 2017 by George Barna[1], the lack of the integration of reported Biblical worldview as it relates to beliefs and behavior is alarming. In the study, when asked, 46% of the adults who claim to have a Biblical worldview, only 10% effectively blended their beliefs and behavior into a Christ-like lifestyle. The survey indicates that the vast majority of Christians separate their spiritual lives from their physical lives. This lack of integration between faith and works outlines the challenges facing the modern Western church. Jesus called His Church to be the salt and light of this world; change-agents that can foster transformation in society. As the culture shifts in its attitude away from morality toward relativism, the strong belief in absolute accountability becomes disputed. The Church must address—head on—the central issues of the day with the wisdom of the Holy Spirit, and each follower must be available to be used with genuine Kingdom power. The lack of vitality seen in the Church today drives home the need to return to the God-given design protocols. Violation of

> The lack of vitality seen in the Church today drives home the need to return to the God-given design protocols.

these protocols has led to a depletion of disciples that are free from psychological, physiological, emotional, and spiritual sickness. There is a call of the Holy Spirit for the believer to become available and useful.

Julia Duin writes in her book, *Quitting Church*, "Much church growth is due to transfers from one church to another."[2] While there has always been a struggle of competition among local churches, it must be kept in mind that there are other factors at play in this transference of numeric growth. Generally, society encourages an individualistic, consumer-driven, customer based, entitled people who continue fostering this trend. The Church must address these deep-seated societal values before the transforming message of the Gospel can be delivered. There is a clear difference between churches growing in numbers and the growth of the capacity of the Church to advance the Kingdom of God.

Before entering the subject of God's Design for Personal and Church Growth, it becomes necessary to give some detailed background of how my research led me on this journey. As the book progresses, the development of practical ways in which individuals and churches can understand and follow God's designs for healthy spiritual life growth will materialize. While the information given in this book may stretch the thinking of some, I intend to lay the groundwork for future development strategy and an all-inclusive work. The instigating of this discussion should be followed up with the application of how these design protocols can be used in the unique church settings. Not only should this book help churches grow, but it should inspire individuals to take their personal situations with God to a deeper level.

"He put all things in subjection under His feet and gave Him as head over all things to the Church, which is His body, the fullness of Him who fills all in all."
Ephesians 1:22

THE FORCE OF THE EMERALD LAND

Embarking on a trip to the world of the church brings with it some Land of Oz-type experiences. The less intuitive and dichotomous reality of the Christian life is one of spiritual mathematics. The life of a follower of Jesus begins and ends with God. The equation looks something like this. The sum of successful Christian life = Alpha + Omega. Let me explain. The ability to live a healthy Christian life is solely dependent upon the reality that it has been created by, sustained by, purchased by, and powered by Christ. Like Dorothy in the Wizard of Oz, it ends where it started. Jesus is the First and the Last; He is the Beginning and the End. The deepest step forward in Christian life is not a step at all; it is resting in the finished work of Jesus. Any movement forward in spiritual growth happens first by understanding the truth that the follower is *NOW* seated in the heavenly realm in Christ Jesus.[3] God has defeated all enemies. It is from this position that the follower of Jesus rests and experiences the love which flows through them towards others. The believer must first know the love of God which surpasses natural knowledge. This love instigated the plan before the beginning of creation. It starts with God and returns to Him.

> Any movement forward in spiritual growth happens first by understanding the truth that the follower is *NOW* seated in the heavenly realm in Christ Jesus.

As people look for that which will fulfill their deepest needs, it is imperative for relevant churches to present this power of a loving Father. As seekers look for a place of hope, power, and purpose, may they find a vibrant church that operates in the fullness of joy found only in the Gospel. Giving hope without purpose and power is not the Gospel at all. Likewise, giving keys to purpose or power without hope is only part of the Good News. It is central for those who lead the church to be watchful over the natural tendency and pull toward making "going to church" an activity that only stimulates or placates the consumer. The tendency toward a self-help driven ideology can become dangerous and

3

counter-productive to God's purpose. The Gospel is not self-help, but self-reduction. The power of the Christian life comes from delighting in God and His completed work of redemption. There is a shocking reaction to the revelation of discovering that "somewhere over the rainbow" is found in the truth that "there is no place like home," in Jesus. A genuine spiritual journey uncovers the truth that Jesus is all that is needed, and He fulfills every desire.

STORMS A COMING

> From the far north, they heard a low wail of the wind, and Uncle Henry and Dorothy could see where the long grass bowed in waves before the storm. There now came a sharp whistling in the air from the south, and as they turned their eyes that way they saw ripples in the grass coming from that direction also. Suddenly, Uncle Henry stood up. "There's a cyclone coming, Em," he called to his wife. "I'll go look after the stock." Then he ran towards the sheds where the cows and horses were kept. Aunt Em dropped her work and came to the door. One glance told her of the danger close at hand. "Quick, Dorothy!" she screamed. "Run for the cellar!"[4]

It says in Matthew 11:12, *And from the days of John the Baptist until now the kingdom of heaven suffers violence, and violent men take it by force.* Just like Dorothy in the grand story of the Wizard of Oz,[5] the advancement of God's kingdom causes a violent reaction as it engages our world. As Dorothy is whisked away to a new world by an act of God, she finds herself on an adventure in much the same way a new believer sets out to lay hold of whatever has gotten a hold of them (Philippians 3:12). This journey, like Dorothy's, leads them to the discovery that they have crushed the enemy, been given supernatural power, and set on a direction to a strange new world called "Church." As the fresh convert sports the newly acquired Gospel shoes (that hold

4

all the power they will ever need), they still have some desire to find the pot of gold at the end of the rainbow. As they look for an Oz that will give them greater power that will take them home, they set out to find a teacher that will lead them on.

While searching for "somewhere over the rainbow," Dorothy collects travel companions. She quickly discovers that the expectations, needs, and wants of her friends are different and unique to each one. They were all looking for somewhere or something different that would fill a deep inner felt want. People have these same distinctions as they approach the Church. As Dorothy sets out to find the solution for her dilemma, the Scarecrow, Tin Woodman, and the Cowardly Lion all have deficits that they expect to have corrected after visiting the Emerald City and the Great and Powerful Oz.[6]

While following the road of yellow brick leading to the land of hope, our friends encounter the Kalidahs[7]—monstrous beasts with bodies like bears and heads like tigers sporting very large sharp claws that threaten the strongest of adversaries. For the follower of Jesus, the road toward the Great City has wild forces also. Christians face these obstacles as they journey spiritually. Two of the greatest struggles they encounter in their walk with Jesus are the feelings of powerlessness and shame. The greatest battle against these two forces has already been won; the disciple must apply the grand victory of the cross and win the clashes of each day. Jesus paid a heavy cost for the believer's freedom and power. It is the duty of all those who disciple others to teach and demonstrate how to overcome the two hindrances of powerlessness and shame. One of the greatest lessons to learn is that it is the love of Christ that is to control the follower, not fear and shame. And it is this lesson that brings with it the greatest freedom and joy.

TRUE GOSPEL

As the early disciples discovered in Luke Chapter 24, the Gospel has no power unless it is experienced in its entirety. As Cleopas and his friend traveled away from the tragedy of the crucifixion of Jesus, they rehearsed the disappointment and fear of the past week's events. They spoke of the high moments and the lows. The disciples recounted the events to each other while a man joined them on their journey. Not knowing it was Jesus the resurrected, they began explaining to Him how disappointing it was that this crucified man failed to bring about the

> The Gospel is not going to make this life easier; it is going to make real life possible.

"over the rainbow" outcome they had expected. They had all the details of the Gospel down to a precise account. However, when they came to the part about the empty tomb, they only could say that they did not see Him. They were talking a lifeless Gospel. Only the fullness of the truth contained in the Gospel allows for the release of God's transforming power. When Jesus fails to meet the incorrect expectations of people, the Gospel is just a story. The complete Gospel delivers the ability to create salvation of the eternal kind. The Gospel is not going to make this life easier; it is going to make real life possible.

As the discussion of the traveling disciples continued, Jesus then began explaining the messianic purpose of Christ and how it was necessary for Him to die to redeem mankind. Jesus opened up the entire Old Testament and spoke of God's plan from the beginning. Once they turned in for the evening and the disciples sat listening to This Man over the dinner meal, Jesus became known to them in a spectacular fashion, and then He vanished. The disciple's spiritual eyes were opened, their Gospel was transformed, and they took off back to Jerusalem. Instantly their Gospel had real power. Now they were saying that Jesus had really risen! The finished work of Jesus now gripped them with a burning heart of joy.[8]

The atmosphere of the local church needs to help foster this life-transforming power. Only this kind of Gospel inspires the heart of the new believer. The Gospel needs to be communicated in its fullness. The only true power of the Church comes because of the finished work of Christ. Conversely, the use of shame-manipulation or heavy-handed authority has no place in the Community of God. As we will see in the section on Leadership, the attitude of the authority structure of the local church is critical. For the Body of Christ to grow and fulfill Her design, the correct leadership structure is necessary. Jesus has so empowered His people that, as Apostle Paul stated, *The God of peace will soon crush Satan under your feet.*[9] The victory of the believer is sure because the vicarious act of Jesus accomplished it on the cross.

In Psalms Chapter 1 the contrast between those with true power and the powerless is clear. The blessed man delights in the law[*] of the Lord, he meditates continually, and the result is being firmly planted with fruit that gives life. He prospers in everything he does. Notice that he is "planted." He is established by God's doing; not by self-effort.

In contrast, the wicked begin by walking. Moving in the path of sinners where he gains temporary power. He "stands" with like-minded manipulators and self-seeking evildoers. He uses earthly power to get needs and desires met. He lastly sits in the seat of his own making which results in ultimate destruction. Christ calls us to sit with Him and let this firm foundation produce life in us. We are to rest from our works and delight in the Creator's powerful competency.

FIRST TIME

In the story of The Wizard of Oz, the traveling companions find that the journey to the Emerald City is filled with people and creatures that help and hinder their progress. At times, people saw the travelers as different and something to be feared. I would imagine that when a guest arrives, for the first time at a new church, there are a few onlookers that create this same feeling of alienation. The church can be a very intimidating place. It is important that the "front door" of the church present a welcoming and safe experience.

As Dorothy and her friends knocked on the gate of the Emerald City, they were only allowed entry to see the Great and Powerful Oz because

---

[*] *"Law" here depicts the messianic plan and direction of God in contrast to the Ten Commandments.*

she had the special shoes and the kiss that sealed her forehead.[10] Dorothy's shoes and the special kiss may represent the Gospel shoes and the seal of the Holy Spirit--a Kingdom person. It is the thinking of some that the weekend experience is just for believers. If the church is called to reach the unchurched, there must be a way to bring the seeker into experiencing the presence of God. As God's family is seen enjoying the Father, the onlooker may discover something that intrigues their soul. Being a part of something so wonderful that transcends the normal earthly life has great appeal for most. The question is, how well is the congregation experiencing this magnificent design? If the foyer is filled with conflict (what I call "trauma/drama"), is this the true reflection of what it is like to be a part of God's earthly family?

GREEN SPECTACLES

As the story of OZ unfolds Dorothy and friends were escorted through the city and made to wear spectacles for their "own protection." The glasses made everything they gazed upon look very green. In church today, there may be so many "special rules" and assumptions that unchurched and de-churched find it to be like the *locking on* of these special glasses. This notion to them is hypercritical and frankly, a little eccentric.

In this story, Oz, the Great and Terrible represents the projected expectation of the people on the leader. As Dorothy and her friends one by one approach Oz, they all encounter a different image of him. He is demanding of all of them and asks things of them he is unwilling to do himself. He leaves the impression that to get something, you must put something in first.

"Well," said the Head, "I will give you my answer. You have no right to expect me to send you back to Kansas unless you do something for me in return. In this country, everyone must pay for everything he gets. If you wish me to use my magic power to send you home again, you must do something for me. Help me, and I will help you."[11]

It is unfortunate that many times in our churches there is this apparent attitude. It may not even be planned, but people hear things that lead them to think that the only reason they can be in attendance is that of their ability to help the pastor or leader achieve his "vision." Intended or not, this perception can destroy a church or cause it to miss her

> The job of leadership is to help each person grow up in Christ and find their designed place in God's grand narrative.

divine call. The Bible teaches that the purpose of the leadership of the Church is for the *equipping of the saints for the work of service, to the building up of the body of Christ; until we all attain to the unity of the faith, and of the knowledge of the Son of God, to a mature man, to the measure of the stature which belongs to the fullness of Christ.*[12] The job of leadership is to help each person grow up in Christ and find their designed place in God's grand narrative.

The expectation of the "somewhere over the rainbow" experience from churches may fall extremely short. Everyone (not just leaders) seems to have some idea of what church should be like and what it should do for them. Faulty expectations put undue pressure upon church leadership to give the people what they imagine. Keeping the direction of the church in line with the mandates of Scripture while being sensitive to the wants, desires, and expectations of the people are the jobs of leadership. The life-giving message of the Bible and the power of transformation cut crosswise against the cultural tide. Breaking unnecessary religious barriers and creating a Spirit-welcoming environment becomes the real task.

In the story of the Wizard of Oz, I perceive an underlying message. The message I discovered is that to experience the "somewhere over the rainbow" place; one must first realize that "there is no place like home." It is important for the Christian to realize that his/her life ended on the cross along with Jesus. On the last day of God creating our universe, He made the man. The man entered into his time of work, but it was God's time of rest. Only after one realizes that the work of God for them, is believing in His Son can real power be released. They have been crucified with Christ, but now they live by faith in this life as they walk for Him.[13]

GOLDEN CALF

When we look at the ministry of Jesus, we often see The Master engaging the people based upon their perceived need at that moment. Jesus always loved people where they were, and He loved them enough not to leave them there. Some try too hard to make the church work for everyone. Jesus would offer His amazing gift, but He never seemed to be concerned about those who just walked away. At times, He put obstacles in front of people to "up the **ante**" which got to the root of their personal motivation. The church should never put a stumbling block in front of anyone; however, it is also not the church's job to create a "golden calf." The creating of calves to appease the masses will always lead to idolatry. This ability to reach people within the framework of their felt needs is never easy. Maintaining a strong conviction that Jesus is the true answer to all of life's issues will empower the leadership to stay clear of presenting manmade ingenuity in place of Gospel power.

It is important to embrace some of the cultural values as long as they do not compromise the teachings of Jesus in any way. I love technology and doing the church services with excellence. RockFish uses a multitude of video projections, monitors, live worship band, enhanced lighting, live feed to Facebook, outdoor third space area where the service is broadcast, apps to communicate sermon notes, and I preach presenting slides from an iPad. All these items enhance the weekend worship experience and, in some cases, allows the seekers that are checking out RockFish to come away with the impression that the church is relevant and understands that there is a world outside of the church where they are seated. RockFish strives to have the best social media presentation available. The website is under constant supervision.

> We want to convey "a taste" of the church before the guest arrives.

We expect to be "checked out" by people looking for a church to attend. We want to convey "a taste" of the church before the guest arrives. Having a visual for the guest to check out does a couple of things. 1) it encourages the person looking for this flavor of church and 2) it helps keep people that do not like our "brand" of church from wasting time visiting and leaving disappointed. The pastors at RockFish try very hard to keep from using special religious language from the front. Our messages are life-application and orbit around the central theme--the Gospel.

In his book, *Christian Wisdom of the Jedi Masters*, Dick Staub makes this statement,

Many who call themselves seekers are in truth dabblers, simply wading ankle-deep and playing on the shore of a vast, limitless ocean. We stay close by the beach, building sand castles, afraid to risk entering the fathomless waters where dwell the risk and rewards of the open sea. We wonder why we cannot catch an exhilarating spiritual wave like a surfer, or acquire a sailor's speed, with anchor up and sails at full mast, billowing with the wind. The pleasures of the ocean are available only to those who go deeper and farther.[14]

Being seeker-sensitive[*] can never mean compromising to the point of offending the righteous and holy God. Jesus stated, *Enter by the narrow gate; for the gate is wide and the way is broad that leads to destruction, and many are those who enter by it. For the gate is small, and the way is narrow that leads to life, and few are those who find it.*[15]

EXPECTATIONS, VALUES, AND PERCEPTIONS

Some of the difficulty lies in definition and assumptions. An example is the tension of a newly married couple when they discover they differ in expectations, values, and communication styles. The local church must

---

[*] *Seeker- a person looking for and open to spiritual truth.*

learn to address and navigate these same issues. As a Certified Christian Marriage and Family Therapist, I find the disparity in these issues between the engaged, and unfortunately, the newly married couple quite challenging. I recall this tension in the early years my marriage. Right after my wife and I had our first child, we had a "discussion" on when and how was the "correct way" to celebrate Christmas. Do you open the presents over several days or is it right to open them all Christmas morning? These unexplored expectations, values, and the lack of communication before the event led to interesting marital insights for my wife and myself. Marriage seems to parallel the issues facing misunderstandings of the purpose of the church. An honest, transparent look at these differences may help the couple avoid bumps in the road ahead, as well as the governmental leadership of a local church.

Whether you are talking about marriage or governance of a church body, unclear vision, expectations, or values most often lead to conflict and division. For a church to grow healthily, the communication and overall acceptance of the purpose of Church is central. The presuppositions of the "what," and the "why" we are doing something are paramount. It is my heart to help clarify and operationally define terms that we use which, at times, have become disconnected from their actual meaning. One major problem can be the assumption that everyone is on the same page, when in fact there may be a great disparity of meaning and understanding of the end goals. In Chapter 2, I will help simplify definitions and how they are used in the context of church growth.

PURPOSEFUL CONNECTION

It is the obligation and duty of the leadership of the Church to help her grow in a healthy manner. A healthy church will grow. However, the true measurement of growth and proper development are known only to God. Healthy things will grow, but not everything that grows is healthy. For example, cancer in the human body grows rapidly and takes up many calories. Obviously, this type of growth is unwanted. Churches can have growth that requires a lot of energy, time and effort, but can produce unwanted results. As leaders, everything must be done in such a way that the spiritual building process is accomplished in a careful/ accountable way. The growth

> Proper growth happens through authentic connection to Jesus.

of a church doesn't happen automatically. Proper growth happens through authentic connection to Jesus. When the application of His mandates to His followers is kept, there is healthy growth. Jesus founded the Church, and He will build the local church if His followers obey the Architect's plans. Rick Warren states, "A great commitment to the great commandment and the great commission will grow a great church."[16] I am the Senior Pastor of RockFish Church in Raeford, North Carolina. At RockFish Church, I have employed these concepts and have seen tremendous results. I highly recommend studying the principles found in Rick's book and applying the principles to your community.

When reading Acts 2, it becomes apparent that the driving force of the early church was focused upon God's purpose. The activities seen in the early church echo the ideas that Rick has captured in his book. A good page, in his book, to get a clear idea on how these activities translate into applied forces in the church are found in the chart on page 119.[17]

In the early days of RockFish, I as the pastor, found myself aiming at nothing and hitting everything except the purpose God intended. This newly formed church needed direction and proper identity. It became important to establish the foundation on purpose rather than copying forms or programs. Finding the church identity created an exciting healthy growth mode. I must interject at this point that RockFish didn't assume all the doctrine, activities, nor personality of Rick Warren's church; but the foundational principles of purpose he articulated drives the church today. It is important to note that you can copy principles but not practices and form. Each church God has begun has its unique call, vision, and expression of purpose. We will go into these in greater detail.

NOT ANOTHER CHURCH!

I was not the founding pastor of Raeford Christian Fellowship (RCF became RockFish Church after relaunching). About two years into the church plant, I was asked to take over due to the Founding Senior Pastor's health. I struggled with the legitimacy of planting a church in Raeford, North Carolina. At that time Raeford was a small southern town with a city population of under 6,000 people, and the entire county population was just over 25,000. The city of Raeford was in a state of negative growth. It seemed like there were churches on every corner. I asked myself the question, "Why another church?" This question led me to discover the call of God on the church and develop a strategy to fulfill that call. As of today, RockFish Church has grown from the original eleven families to nearly 3,000 members. I learned that God loves people, and He will do whatever it takes to reach them. I have been asked by other local church pastors what our "secret sauce" was. I must say that building the church on the foundation that had already been laid by Jesus, and keeping the main thing, the main thing, has helped sustain us in God's intended direction.

My heart was and is motivated to take the Gospel where it has not been. As I found myself serving a church in an area that seemed saturated with established works located in the Bible-belt of the South, my desire for validity before God came to the forefront. Because of the nearness to Fort Bragg,* another factor needed to be overcome. The military turnover rate presented its challenges. The movement of army personnel from and to Fort Bragg created a constant revolving door of new people and the loss of established church members. The rate of loss in any given year could be as high as 25%. Growing a church within this consistent depletion of people meant the church needed to clarify and communicate the vision relentlessly.

One great benefit of having a church in the military environment of

---

* *Fort Bragg is a United States Army base that hosts the 18th Airborne Corp, FORSCOM, 82nd Airborne Division, and Special Operations Forces.*

Fort Bragg's "backdoor" is the international feel of the congregation. People come to this area from all over the country and world. They come from a wide range of background and religious experiences. As a pastor, I found myself serving the greatest people on the planet. The heart of service members and their families truly exemplify the true understanding of, *Greater love has no man than this, that one lay his life down for his friends.*[18] In this aspect, the military mindset goes hand in hand with the servant leadership model Jesus taught. This dynamic led to three value distinctions for RockFish Church; dads, moms, and children all worshipping together, a multicultural congregation, and focused support of the military personnel and their families. Working with families as they navigate military life and hardships proved to be challenging and rewarding. My background as a Certified Christian Marriage and Family Therapist along with my education in multicultural psychology proved to be a good asset.

In his book, *The Unchurched Next Door,* Thom Rainer states, per his research, "Eight out of ten unchurched persons said they would come to church if they were invited."[19] Several questions then must be answered, 1) what is the church and what responsibility does it have when the unchurched person accepts the invite? (Rainer makes the case that there are 160 million unchurched in America.)[20] 2) Why is the church so unsuccessful in reaching these souls with the power of the Gospel in a once "Christian nation" and, 3) why does the average believer find it so hard to ask a person to church?

On the last question, Thom suggests that "In the postmodern culture of twenty-first-century America, Christians may as well accept that the criticisms of intolerance will continue. The greater concern is that many Christians are unwilling to take a narrow Biblical view because they do not want to be regarded as intolerant."[21] I

> Much of the historical purpose of the Church has led to a tension between church being a place where believers go to worship God and a place where people can be introduced to God and His people.

think this may be true to some extent; however, there may be deeper obstacles hindering the average believer from asking people to church. In Chapter 3, we will explore some of the philosophical assumptions relating to the purpose of "going to church." Much of the historical purpose of the Church has led to a tension between church being a place where believers go to worship God and a place where people can be introduced to God and His people.

FOUNDATIONS

"I know that everything God does will remain forever;
there is nothing to add to it and there is nothing to take
from it, for God has so worked that man should fear Him."
Ecclesiastes 3:14

The start of a matter, the beginning, the outset, the origin; will, to a great degree, determine the outcome. I once took a notion to hike part of the Appalachian Trail or "A.T." as it is known. My part of the trail began at Bear Creek in the beautiful Great Smoky Mountains of North Carolina. The trails were well marked IF you knew some simple rules. For instance, the symbol for "Appalachian Trail" is this:

I mistook this symbol for an arrow pointing forward, and I ended up a long way from my intended destination. I walked for eleven miles (up)

never finding my planned camping spot. It is very dangerous to camp outside of the provided shelters, and the Forestry Service forbids it (mostly because of a large black bear population). Not only was I lost, but also it began to rain for the rest of the backpacking day. I was forced to pitch my tent on the side of a trail, on a sharply sloping, weed-infested piece of ground. That night, as my tent filled with water, I wondered why I ever wanted to leave my warm home, wife, and bed to come to this place to be so miserable.

However, the next day I awoke to a crisp morning and the sound of water rushing far below in the canyon. I understood then where the mountains derived their name. Beautiful white smoke rose from the green slopes all around me. The air smelled clean and fresh as the newborn sun began its life across the Carolina blue sky. At this point, I felt as though I did arrive at the spot God intended for me. This, and the knowledge that the next eleven miles were *all downhill* back the way I came, gave me the feeling of being in the right place at the right time.

Beginning any work with the correct foundation is important. *For no man can lay a foundation other than the one which is laid, which is Jesus Christ.*[22] It is surprising to me to see so much of the Christian work and life built on other things than the foundation that Christ gave. Traditions, personality, programs, and convenience have caused the collapse of many works and lives. Understanding how the church got where it is becomes extremely important. The source of destruction of any organization is present in its foundation. Jesus directed His followers exactly how to lay this foundation and how He intends to build upon it. The work of Christ has no limits, and nothing can stop its advancement when Jesus is the One building.

And He came and preached peace to you who were far away, and peace to those who were near; for through Him we both have our access in one Spirit to the Father. So then you are no longer strangers and aliens, but you are fellow citizens with the saints, and are of God's household, having been built on the foundation of the apostles and prophets, Christ Jesus Himself being the

*cornerstone, in whom the whole building, being fitted together,
is growing into a holy temple in the Lord, in whom you also are
being built together into a dwelling of God in the Spirit.*[23]

This passage from Ephesians Chapter 2 holds the foundational secret to a healthy church which is peace. The whole divine purpose of Christ coming to earth was to bring restoration of a broken relationship between the created and the Creator. Not only did Christ bring forgiveness, but empowerment to the creature of the full adopted relationship into the Holy Family. Making into one, a people for God's own possession is at the heart of God's desire. The Father always wanted children, and through the sacrifice of God's only Begotten, He has many sons and daughters. This is the Gospel. As Matt Chandler puts it,

And that's a huge difference—the difference between knowing the gospel and being consumed by the gospel, being defined by the gospel, being driven by the gospel. It's one thing to see the gospel as an important facet of one's ministry. It's quite another to hold firmly to it as the centerpiece for all a church is and does, to completely orbit around it.[24]

It is interesting to note that in Chandler's book, the word "gospel" is used 566 times! It is also remarkable that the Name of Jesus is used 410 times! He drives home the centrality of Jesus and His Gospel.

STATEMENTS THAT GUIDE THE SHIP

The vision statement of RockFish Church is, "To see a radically abandoned people given to the advancement of the Gospel." Its mission statement is, "To build an unstoppable church on the foundation of Jesus." As you can see, the premise for the church all hinges upon the finished work of Jesus. As we then labor, we do so within the framework of the understanding that Jesus is forming His Church. He does so through the direction of His Word and the power of the Gospel. These twin concepts guide everything the church does in ministry. Any ministry philosophy that flows from a solid foundation of the teachings of Jesus and the power of the Gospel results in the successful day to day outworking of the church's actions.

> As we then labor, we do so within the framework of the understanding that Jesus is forming His Church.

The Church must respond to the authority of Jesus with all seriousness. Jesus made the functional outworking activity of the Church clear in Mark 16. Jesus commands, *Go into all the world and preach the Gospel to all creation. He who has believed and is baptized shall be saved; but he who has disbelieved shall be condemned.*[25] Again, in Mathew 28 He directs,

> *All authority has been given to Me in heaven and on earth. Go therefore and make disciples of all the nations, baptizing them in the name of the Father and the Son and the Holy Spirit, teaching them to observe all that I commanded you; and lo, I am with you always, even to the end of the age.*[26]

The sheer magnitude, absolute nature, the all life encompassing, and priority of this command becomes the greatest challenge throughout the history of humanity. Jesus stated that the trigger for the end of the age would be the fulfillment of His commission.[27] The ultimate standard of a spiritually mature church and the individual is measured against the obedience to these words of Jesus. The current world grows darker and darker while many followers of Jesus lay asleep in the poppy fields of Oz.

The intoxication of Western civilization with its draw toward comfort and self-sufficiency has cradled much of the Church into a spiritual slumber. Currently, the doors of opportunity to reach into the darkest of places are wide open. The challenge and questions remain: will the people of God become the force He intended to get the job done and usher in the return of Christ? Another question of importance is, will the people of God be able to *come out of the world system*?[28] Will they be spiritually, emotionally, mentally, and physically strong enough to complete the Great Commission mandated by Christ? Will God's children be available and usable for the long-haul? Do the followers of Jesus believe and act as if they have been called to be the temple of the indwelling Holy Spirit? May the grace of God empower His people to become all He intended. In the chapters ahead, it will become obvious that to love God with everything; it is imperative that a holistic stewardship approach of the body, soul, and spirit be taken. The call of Jesus to discipleship is a call to the total relinquishing of all parts of the follower's life. *He who has found his life will lose it, and he who has lost his life for My sake will find it.*[29]

MINISTRY PHILOSOPHY

Ministry philosophy leads to the practical outworking of life endeavors. Philosophy answers the question of why the effort is employed to attain a specific goal. When Jesus commanded His disciples to "Go," it is unclear exactly where He wanted each of His followers to go. Ministry philosophy stands directly on top of theology and asks the question, how does this apply to the given situation, culture, people and resource-matches available? The specificity of the practical outworking accomplishments, as they relate to ministry philosophy, stand connected directly on top. Good theology and proper ministry philosophy results in clear direction and functional life flow. Wisdom is the knowledge of what principle to apply when. Good principles, without wisdom, end up being a pile of building materials with no shape. Good theology, with good ministry philosophy, gives a clear direction for the practical activities of a church. The transferring of vision and mission to the church will put clarity and focus that will energize the pursuits of its members. As you journey through this book, I pray that these guiding principles will become apparent.

2

DEFINITIONS

2.1 INTRODUCTION

Words spoken by God gave birth to the universe. It was the Word that became flesh and dwelt among us. Words may convey truth or lies. Debates are won or lost because of words. Wars have been started because of words. Words build up or tear down. Lives have been ruined, and marriages have been devastated with the use of words. Words invoke anger or incite emotional attachment. We will all be judged because of the words we use.[30]

I have included this section to help clarify and have our thoughts converge on, what I believe, to be one of the most important topics of our generation: communication. Communication, both verbal and non-verbal, have the power to change relational dynamics. The Scripture states: *be transformed by the renewing of your mind.*[31] It is important to note that the effects of interpersonal neurobiology[*] through the communication of thoughts can have significant transformative outcomes. According to Curt Thompson, "A working description of the mind is an embodied and relational process that emerges from within and between brains whose task it is to regulate the flow of energy and information."[32] Notice the movement "between brains." As you read the words contained in this book, thoughts produced by the words cause energy to

---

[*] *Interpersonal Neurobiology (IPNB) a term coined by Dr. Dan Siegel that explains the way the brain grows and is influenced by personal relationships.*

flow. It becomes imperative then that the terms used are clarified to avoid misunderstanding and to result in helpful outcomes. As I move through the rest of this book, I will endeavor to operationally define critical terms and display them at the bottom of each page for easy reference. (I have also included these terms in Appendix A3 in the back of the book for easy reference).

2.2 CONNECTION

As a preacher of God's Word, when crafting a message, it becomes apparent that word choices are significant. It is by the preaching of the Gospel that the power of God is released.[33] Notice that when God's words are joined with the action of preaching, God's power is released. It is not simply enough to use Bible words; these words must be incarnational. As Jesus became flesh through the incarnation, we must live in such a way as to demonstrate to the people in our surrounding culture the reality of the words we are using. It's not enough in today's Western culture to say words arranged in a logical, Biblical, proof-text outline. There are all kinds of communications coming from many different directions, and many of these lines of communication are not in agreement. Any subject can be looked up on Google or demonstrated on YouTube. One of the emotional needs of the post-modern world is the need to connect, to understand, and to be understood. This type of connection is one of the greatest challenges for the Church today.

> It is not simply enough to use Bible words; these words must be incarnational.

Words matter, but words with the connection are life-changing. In the story of Abraham, Sarai, and Hagar; Hagar gave God a name after He promised to bless her and her child. *She called the name of the Lord who spoke to her, "Thou art a God who sees"; for she said, "Have I even remained alive here after seeing Him?"*[34] The soul loves to be understood and to understand. To know and be known by God creates a spiritual linking that draws people toward Christ. The Scripture is powerful and will touch every human need at the deepest level when it is communicated with connectivity. Transparency, honesty, and relatability become the most important tool for leadership operation.

It is also important to stress that using words to trigger emotional responses just for this purpose alone, must be carefully avoided. The Scriptures teach that *For in Christ Jesus neither circumcision nor uncircumcision means anything, but faith working through love.*[35] When it becomes apparent that a church is using manipulation tactics to persuade people to behavioral change, quick correction is needed. The only true and proper motivational force appropriate to be used is "faith working through love." For example, it becomes an easy ploy to shame people or promise a "blessing" for serving. The goal of serving is not guilt relief or repayment to Jesus but giving service because of faith working through love. We can only have this type of love through the knowledge of being supremely loved by Jesus. His love is the motivation and source of anything worthwhile that comes from us. It is clear when reading 1 Corinthians 13 that without love nothing counts and there is no benefit at all even in the greatest feat or grandest exploit. Love is the connection. God is the source. We are to decrease, and He is to increase. And, when we reduce self, we can truly love the way Christ loves.

2.3 G.R.O.W.T.H.

"For we are His workmanship, created in Christ Jesus for good works, which God prepared beforehand, that we should walk in them."
Ephesians 2:10

I developed a spiritual growth roadmap that has helped me in my personal and leadership roles while serving RockFish church. I have discovered that the same spiritual growth principles that help me in my walk with Jesus can be applied to leading the local church. Spiritual growth is just that; spiritual growth—no matter how you apply it.

Scriptural principles never change. The practices may be different, but the principles remain the same. God's principles bring true spiritual formation.

The enhancement of spiritual formation is directly related to the healthiness of one's walk with Jesus and the culture of the local church. According to Dallas Willard,

> Spiritual formation could become a term for those processes through which people are inwardly transformed in such a way that the personality and deeds of Jesus Christ naturally flow out from them when and wherever they are. In other words, it can be understood as the process by which true Christlikeness is established in the very depths of our being. Thus, multitudes of men and women could be brought forth from generation to generation to be Christ's redemptive community: the true 'city set on a hill,' of which Jesus spoke that had been established in the midst of earth now as it shall be for eternity in the midst of the cosmos. We could become a true 'society of Jesus.' We could be the life-transforming salt and light in a darkened world which God has always intended His covenant people to be.[36]

It is important to note that it is impossible to have a strong corporate structure if the individuals are not moving toward healthy spiritual lives.

There is a tendency to oversimplify and be reductionistic in our approach to spiritual development and the Body of Christ. However, the interplay of all facets of human experience must be considered. For example, the personal state of feeling depressed often is a complex symptom that could result from varying causes. The causation factors for depression can vary from life situations, loss, spiritual repercussions, biochemical or hormonal imbalances, diet, or neurological causes. In this same way, human spiritual growth factors must encompass all areas of life: body, soul, and spirit. To overlook the physical body and underestimate the importance of natural health factors would be a mistake. Personal spiritual health, as well as the health of the Body of

Christ, is interconnected to all parts of life. It is important to say here that it is not my intention to address all the aspects of human health. However, it is extremely important for all leaders to consider body, soul, and spirit issues as they relate to individuals, as well as, to the whole of the church.

> However, it is extremely important for all leaders to consider body, soul, and spirit issues as they relate to individuals, as well as, to the whole of the church.

The natural body grows in a healthy fashion based upon natural daily activities. Many studies have resulted in the discovery that there are seven main areas of human behavior that are correlated to good physical health. Without careful attention to all seven areas, the human body will eventually become unhealthy — the combination of proper applications of sleep, margin, avoiding toxic exposure, diet, relationships, water, and exercise results in health benefits and longevity. It has become apparent in Western culture that as these health factors are ignored the results are devastating. The shocking amount of overweight, overstressed, out of shape, and sick people is staggering. The trends of our Post-modern Western culture will quickly hit the tipping thresholds of human disaster. Physical health is connected to spiritual health.

The acrostic, G.R.O.W.T.H., stands for the spiritual principles that will guide most of the rest of the book and is the fundamental reason for the healthy growth in the individual as well as the church. These principles are founded squarely upon scriptural ideologies. The foundation of all truth must be rooted and grounded upon God's Holy Word. All philosophical structures must rest directly upon this foundation. The practical application, however, may differ functionally as everyday situations arise. Most problems arise not in the theological arena but when principles are cross-applied to different venues or missional targets. It is important to restate that the wrong application of good practice can be devastating. The practical function of these principles may also be changed given the need of the unique circumstance.

The first letter, "G" (in the acrostic G.R.O.W.T.H.), stands for, "Gospel God." The foundational premise of this letter is that the Gospel is God's plan, source, connection, center, and generator of all spiritual health. Second, the "R" represents "Response Repentance" which is the action needed on our part for a human to change. The "O" stands for "Omega Optics" which explains the need for focused connection vertically toward God and horizontally toward others. Next, the "W" stands for "Worship Wonders" which emphasizes the factors of worship upon the human heart that creates the outworking of virtue. The letter "T" gives meaning and direction to the idea of structuring for growth through the "Theocratic Tapestry": a power configuration which guides the process of power distribution to help the person being served and to fulfill the vision. Lastly, the letter "H" clarifies the need for a philosophy of an overall "Healthy Home," which speaks of living day to day within this modern culture.

2.4 ENGAGEMENT: ATTRACT FOR MISSION

Spiritual warfare is to be expected whenever the advancement of God's Kingdom is the aim and direction of any pragmatic endeavor. We are reminded by Apostle Paul that, *Our struggle is not against flesh and blood, but against the rulers, against the powers, against the world forces of this darkness, against the spiritual forces of wickedness in the heavenly places.*[37] Not only does this mean the enemy will resist us as we reach people with the Good News, but will also push back when we work to bring the Gospel forward to redeem culture.

> Likewise, each church has a specific assignment and the tools needed to reach the culture where they reside.

Jesus has called us away from sin to Himself. He has also called us to be a part of reaching all peoples, tongues, tribes, and nations. Reaching means, we must find a way to engage the culture in which we are involved. All believers are called to a people, and God has given us all a platform to reach them. Likewise, each church has a specific assignment and the tools needed to reach the culture where they reside. Cultural and Biblical standards put the activity of church between two forces that must be held, addressed, and conquered; the tension that lies between being attractional and missional. These two forces must be addressed. The success or failure of the spiritual life of the church will depend largely upon the fruitful outcome of defining and operating in this tension.

Jesus was always on a mission; however, He attracted people to His message by affirming certain cultural values. I am not saying this is a straightforward or easy task to achieve, but the followers of Jesus must learn to navigate these issues with great wisdom. Speaking to, using, and affirming cultural values and norms without compromising Christ's teachings becomes the challenge of the day. Extremes in either direction will result in legalism or license.

My definition of being "missional" is the ability of a person or church to be used, empowered, and directed by Jesus to reach people. It is clear from reading the New Testament that Jesus has called His people to go everywhere proclaiming the Good News. They were instructed to make followers, teach, and to baptize those who believe and repent. These activities of the church are clearly stated and demonstrated throughout the early church teachings. The individual and the church must be on mission to be truly obedient followers of the Lord. Reaching, teaching, preaching, discipling, worshiping, and gathering are the authentic activities of the church. This mandate carries the weight of responsibility for every follower to find his or her place in the Body of Christ.

Being a voice for the Gospel that can be clearly understood within the context of a culture, in such a way that there are not unnecessary hindrances that obstruct the message, is part of the responsibility of every believer. The religious leaders of Jesus' day were warned about putting requirements and stumbling blocks in front of the people. According to Jesus, they were, *"Making them twice as fit for hell as themselves."*[38] This is not to say that the offensive nature of the message of Christ that happens because of the message itself is neutralized. The challenge is to find a way to speak to people so as not to unnecessarily offend them but to uphold—without compromise—the teachings of Jesus.

Being "attractional" is the ability of a follower or church to attract seekers within the culture into an experience that will allow the Holy Spirit to point to Jesus. To be a church that is attractional, the religious barriers that are not of God must be removed. These barriers include the use of man-made traditions that repel the unbeliever. Religious language, dress codes, worship actions, programs, modalities, and manipulations must be explored, identified and removed. Paul instructed the church in Corinth that the church was to use its power to edify not confuse. *If therefore the whole church should assemble together, and all speak in tongues, and ungifted men or unbelievers enter, will they say that you are mad?*[39] However, when the power of the Holy Spirit moves, we should not forbid Him or be ashamed of His working. It is clear from the entire 14th chapter of 1 Corinthians that the Holy Spirit is present and working to edify. The issue in this passage is underscoring the importance of edification.

The role of church leadership structure becomes crucial in the navigation of the how, why and where of cultural integration and missional trueness. The church leaders must make every effort to create a church culture that protects the mission of the church while removing needless obstacles for unbelievers. In chapter 7, the importance of the proper leadership structure and its use in this area will be explored. In their book, "Creature of the Word," Matt Chandler, Josh Patterson, and Eric Geiger quote Gailyn Van Rheenen, concerning becoming too accommodating to the culture, as saying,

> The church leaders must make every effort to create a church culture that protects the mission of the church while removing needless obstacles for unbelievers.

Syncretism occurs when Christian leaders accommodate, either consciously or unconsciously, to the prevailing plausibility structures or worldviews of their culture. Syncretism, then, is the conscious or unconscious reshaping of Christian plausibility structures, beliefs, and practices through cultural accommodation so that they reflect those of the dominant culture. Or stated in other terms, syncretism is the blending of Christian beliefs and practices with those of the dominant culture so that Christianity loses it distinctiveness and speaks with a voice reflective of its culture.[40]

Moreover, it is important to note that it is imperative for all believers in Christ to make an honest assessment of their personal lives as it relates to syncretism. Likewise, unnecessary religious jargon, traditions, rules, and complex theological concepts must be avoided. The freeing aspects of the Gospel bring spiritual health and growth when understood. Freedom in Christ is a powerful thing. Displaying a heart that handles the truth and fosters health becomes the very "salt" Jesus talks about in the Scripture. As the follower brings his/her being to Jesus to be pruned and corrected, others become spiritually hungry for the authentic life found in Christ.

Successful engagement of the culture, while upholding the full teachings of Jesus, is both the challenge and the reward for the church today. Avoidance of the two extremes of "making golden calves" and legalistic religiosity brings the result of a correct environment for healthy spiritual growth. A cursory study of church history reveals these two problems the church has had to overcome. When either being exclusively missional or attractional, the result is always the same: The Church must maintain the proper balance of grace and truth to maintain spiritual health. The only time the Church grows healthily is when the true Gospel of God is preached, lived, and encouraged.

3

G. R. O. W. T. H. –
GOSPEL GOD

3.1 HEALTHY LIFE SOURCE

also say to you that you are Peter, and upon this rock I (Jesus) will build My church; and the gates of Hades will not overpower it."
Matthew 16:18

According to Rick Warren:

All living things grow-you don't have to make them grow. It's the natural thing for living organisms to do if they are healthy. For example, I don't have to command my three children to grow. They naturally grow. As long as I remove hindrances such as poor nutrition or an unsafe environment, their growth will be automatic. If my kids don't grow, something has gone terribly wrong. Lack of growth usually indicates an unhealthy situation, possibly a disease. In the same way, since the church is a living organism, it is natural for it to grow if it is healthy. The church is a body, not a business. It is an organism, not an organization. It is alive. If a church is not growing, it is dying.[41]

There are many similarities between spiritual and physical health. Pastor Rick states the importance of purpose in the spiritual life of the individual as well as the church. I have used many of the principles found in his book, The Purpose Driven Church.[42] These principles have become the foundation of assimilation at RockFish Church. However, I have discovered that the spiritual health of RockFish included a greater number of principles than the discovery of church and individual purpose alone.

As a Certified Christian Marriage and Family Therapist for over twenty years, I see the needs of the individual as well as the church, to be multifaceted and a bit more complex than the discovery of purpose by itself. I think some other important factors must be recognized before a healthy spiritual life can be realized. It is possible that these concepts might be taken for granted; however, if spiritual health is to be realized, we must lay aside assumptions. To cross-apply spiritual health to varying church-cultural situations, deep consideration as to what makes health must be fully understood. As we have seen in our current Western culture, the "givens are gone." For example, we would expect that all churches believe that the Bible is the final authority for truth; however, cultural relativism and secular humanism have eroded the most commonsense rendering of God's Word.

The teachings throughout all the Scriptures, as they relate to the main Commandments and focus, have always been to love the Lord with all your heart, and with all your soul, and with all your strength, and with all your mind; and your neighbor as yourself.[43] Loving God and loving people with body, soul, and spirit is the key to spiritual health. Loving goes beyond the isolated meaning of our sense of purpose. Loving God and loving others define our purpose as individuals and as a church; but, to fulfill this call and become healthy, the unspoken factors must be addressed.

> There is a difference between doing your purpose and being fulfilled in your purpose.

There is a difference between doing your purpose and being fulfilled in your purpose. Jesus calls His people to be producers not merely doers. His children are to produce from a reality sourced in a deep relationship with the Holy Spirit. Doing purpose and being fulfilled in it is akin to the interplay between faith and works. Simply finding your purpose and doing it will not, in and of itself, insure spiritual fulfillment. This contrast of purpose applies both to an individual and to the Church. The underpinning of the proper context of purpose will be explored in the following chapters. Without a clear understanding of what makes church or individuals healthy, false assumptions result, and the goal of healthy growth will not be realized.

To demonstrate this concept, let's look at the purpose of marriage. Some legitimate purposes for marriage are intimacy, procreation, a platform for ministry and the passing of blessing on to the next generation. As we consider the topic of intimacy in marriage, the different levels of intimacy come into play. Five areas of intimacy form a spoke around the hub of oneness. Not everyone goes into marriage with the same expectations or desires for intimacy in all five. However, for a marriage to find completeness and healthy unity, all five intimacies must be matured. The multifaceted nature of marital oneness exemplifies this complexity.

The first aspect of intimacy has to do with affiliation. I call this social intimacy. Whenever a new relationship is formed that is headed toward marriage, the social network of each partner must be examined. The values of both partners must come into agreement for true social intimacy to happen. For example, do both parties agree that opposite-sex friendships are still appropriate? If these values conflict, the engagement season, as well as the marriage, will suffer. Due to changing concepts, values, and expectations, the social intimacy issues are increasingly a point of contention. For healthy unity between couples, social affiliation and agreement must be achieved.

The next important intimacy factor that needs to be formed is intellectual intimacy. Although there are different types of intellects, for the sake of this illustration, I will group them into overall intelligence. If a couple is preparing for marriage and there is a perceived disparity in IQ between the couple, this difference may result in feelings of unworthiness or superiority. In the past years, I have explored this issue with couples by asking them which one is "smarter." The answer to this question varies widely. I have seen every combination of results. The light this question provides may illuminate what I call the Relation

Selection Principle (RSP) violations. The principle fundamentally says, "birds of a feather flock together." Meaning, if I see a huge perceived difference in intellect, for example, this may indicate a possible major future problem for the couple. I have found that if this root problem is explored, the discovery of a co-dependent, unhealthy relationship, and domination and abuse, may be uncovered. Healthy intellectual intimacy results in mutual satisfaction and potential for joint growth. It's not so much the actual intellectual disparity but the perception of superiority and inferiority.

Thirdly, emotional intimacy, in our example, must also be healthy for there to be complete oneness. Whenever emotional intimacy fails in a relationship, it leaves both parties feeling empty. The internal needs of the individual left unmet pull apart the very fabric of the relationship. The key in correcting this lack of emotional "tank filling" lies in the clarification of just how each partner receives validation. All individuals have basic heart needs. These needs break down into four categories: 1) safety,[*] 2) purpose, 3) value and 4) hope.[†] The intricacies of these four heart needs are complicated, but suffice to say, these are the basic needs of the human heart. Communicating so the other party can receive what is intended is key. Healthy emotional intimacy gives the relationship the power to draw, in ever increasing measures into unity and oneness.

Next is a very important area of physical intimacy. Physical intimacy is one of the favorite areas of the enemy (Satan) used to divide a couple. A myriad of problems can arise in this critical part of the marriage experience. This list is just some of the challenges and obstacles to becoming physically intimate:

---

[*] *Safety relates to the physical, emotional, spiritual, areas of self. The perceived threat to the prime directive of survival may result in freeze, fight, flight, fail, or pacifying behaviors.*

[†] *Hope is the anticipation of future based upon past experience. The unwanted response caused by the "waiting for the other shoe to drop" thought process. Negativity and hopelessness damage and prevent the healing process of the soul.*

- Value Differences
- Perceptions
- Failed or differing expectations
- Physical/medical issues
- Seasons of ebbs and flows
- Psychological / emotional flash-freeze points
- Unforgiveness
- Rhythms between the two
- Drive differences
- Energy
- Life stresses
- Time availability
- Sleep problems
- Medications
- Poor diet
- Lack of proper exercise

Societal pressure, parental expectations, cultural values, religious influences, and the demands of life can heavily impact couples.

As you can see, this is a complicated and powerful area of intimacy. The goal of this section is not to explain all the dynamics of intimacy but to demonstrate the complexities of interpersonal purpose. This example serves as thought provocation.

Lastly, let's look at the dimension of spiritual intimacy. Spiritual intimacy often is the most difficult place in a marriage for a couple to experience oneness. The main reason most couples never enter unity spiritually is a feeling of vulnerability. Exposing one's deepest part is frightening and disarming. Self-protection began in the Garden of Eden and is alive and well today. Most couples hold back this part for fear of their partner gaining an advantage. Becoming transparent before God is one thing, but having another human observe and possibly judge you, is another. Inadequacy, failure, and the possibility to be misunderstood hold many couples back from going to God together in the fullest sense.

Couples that have discovered the joy of spiritual intimacy have a transparent relationship that enables true oneness.

As we have seen in the previous example, the purpose of oneness in marriage is complicated. Other factors lead to a healthy life that transcends purpose alone. The same way plants depend on proper soil, water, temperature, and sunlight; human soul depends upon the proper soil of the water of the Truth of God, the temperature of interpersonal relationships, and the "Sonlight" of God's Holy Spirit. Growing anything healthy, the proper nutrition and growth elements must be present. It is logical to assume, by providing the proper environment and interactions, the plant will grow and produce its purpose. Discovery of purpose, in and of itself, will not ensure a healthy spiritual life.

> Discovery of purpose, in and of itself, will not ensure a healthy spiritual life.

Jesus is the life source; apart from Him, we can do nothing. It may seem overly simplistic, but the Gospel of God must be the foundation of any healthy spiritual growth. Repentance from sin and faith toward God, through the knowledge provided in His teachings, give the only hope for a person and the Church. All life must begin and stay grounded upon this principle. The Gospel makes the Church and sustains the Church. Repentance, like faith, is not exclusively a beginning point or entrance. Repentance is as necessary as inhaling and exhaling. A person or church that leaves the teachings of Christ to "go deeper" has forgotten the Gospel is the power of God and is beyond deep. Leaving the Gospel for the deeper life is like trying to run a marathon without breathing.

In Creature of the Word, Matt Chandler explains:

And this is why the church succeeds, maturing by the power of God's Spirit working in and through the Word as He massages it deeply into the life of His body. A church is alive and full when she is sustained by the sacrifice and resurrection of Christ and is drawn back to that precious reality, again and again, every time she gathers. So... if challenged to give an answer for why we've lost a great deal of our power as the church, one of the major reasons we'd give is this: our understanding about what the Gospel actually does. We seem to have developed Gospel amnesia, forgetting that the Gospel not only creates and sustains the Church but also deeply shapes the Church. Present and future.[44]

Leaving the teachings of Jesus, and the power demonstrated by His life will only lead to an unhealthy life and church. Our philosophies and practices must be placed squarely upon this foundation. As the western culture drifts further away from the simplicity of devotion to Christ and His commands, the results become evident. The book of Romans speaks to this issue and warns of deviant behavior as His truth and lordship are exchanged for worldly affirmations.[45] A stance of not compromising the Gospel message and its life source is mandatory for true spiritual health.

The Gospel must be integrated throughout the entire spectrum of the Church and life. If it becomes "only the starting point" for spiritual life and not the only power-source for spiritual growth, the church will soon be taken away into human-powered Christianity, leading to the Scriptural error. The mature leader understands his power and life comes through the Gospel, and remains vigilant, protecting his/her walk. Many have left the Good News for "deep" revelations and teachings that have caused

> It is extremely important to allow the teachings of Jesus to justify, sustain, and sanctify the follower's entire life.

great harm to the Body of Christ. It is extremely important to allow the teachings of Jesus to justify, sustain, and sanctify the follower's entire life. The human soul was designed to operate in connection with this reality. All theology, philosophy, and practice must line up squarely upon the revelation of the Gospel.

According to Matt Chandler:

In its simplest form, the Gospel is God's reconciling work in Christ-that through the life, death, and resurrection of Christ; God is making all things new both personally for those who repent and believe, and cosmically as He redeems culture and creation from its subjection to futility. The Gospel also forms the church.[46]

The leadership of RockFish Church has taken the stand that Gospel centrality must be consistently evaluated and reinforced throughout the entire ministry. We have fought the pull to give "deeper" teaching that would take away from this held value. We have not been opposed to in-depth theological study, but have continued keeping the main thing, the main thing. The Great Commission has been the grid that guides our main values and decisions. As I am writing this, RockFish Church is engaged in a campaign offering baptism twenty-four hours a day, seven days a week. Keeping the commands of Jesus to go into all the world and baptize has developed into a "baptism culture." The excitement and spiritual health this effort has brought have been invaluable. The unity of the leadership is paramount in this regard. Later in this chapter, the subject of the leadership role in forming the "bones" of the church will make their role apparent.

God has called all His people to integrate the Gospel into all facets of their experience. The saying goes, "the life is in the blood," and for the believer, this is clearly taught throughout Scripture. The sacrifice of Christ on the cross and His blood spilled for all mankind has provided the only way to life. Without His blood, there is no life. It is through the sacrifice of Jesus that the relationship between the Creator and the creature is restored. Christ died for all humanity and paid the price in full. The rejection of this reconciliatory offer ensures the creature remaining in the permanent state of death, separated from God in eternal torment. The Bible teaches, not only that God created all, but He sent His Son to live,

> God has called all His people to integrate the Gospel into all facets of their experience.

teach, satisfy all the law, die to pay for our lives, and rise to defeat death on our behalf. The Gospel is great news indeed! It is the privilege of every believer to tell, point to, and live out this story. As the follower, as well as the Church "seeks first the kingdom" priorities, the life of God is perpetuated.

A LIFE WORTH LIVING

Life in God not only includes longevity but quality. Jesus came to give us life and that life is to be filled with abundance. The teachings of Christ not only sustain the Church, but it grows the Church. As the believers jointly grow, the outcome is life in abundance. A church that is not spiritually growing is a church that has deviated from the Gospel —leaving her first love. The church produces life; not through structures and programs, but through the lived-out knowledge that it is loved first by God, and He called His Body into existence. Love is only produced in the human experience by the revelation of the Savior's first love. *We love because He first loved us.*[47] All activity, no matter how seemingly benevolent, done apart from love, means nothing.[48] The church that goes to the world with God's Gospel must go in love. The growth activity of any church must be grounded in the reality of the Gospel God of Love.

Life, as we know it, has no meaning without the life-giving power of the Gospel. Our giving Creator so loved us that He sent His only begotten Son, to not only reconnect us to Himself but by His blood make us able to receive His Holy Spirit. *Christ redeemed us from the curse of the Law, having become a curse for us… in order that in Christ Jesus the blessing of Abraham might come to the Gentiles,* so that *we might receive the promise of the Spirit through faith.*[49]

Did you catch that? According to this scripture, by Jesus becoming a curse for us, we are now in a state to receive the Holy Spirit! God not only saved us from the wrath to come, but He grants us the new birth to become one with Him as sons and daughters! God has chosen to join us in our everyday existence and activities. To experience true spiritual growth and life, we are to depend on and follow the Holy Spirit.

Becoming the dwelling place of the Holy Spirit is a challenging thought. It seems that much of the Christian's experience in the Western culture is having the Holy Spirit follow them around asking Him to bless what they are doing rather than following Him in His blessing. To experience true spiritual growth, it becomes imperative for the follower to follow the leading of the Holy Spirit.

Following the Holy Spirit is the normal way for Christ-followers to live. If you live for yourself and are powered by yourself, death results; but those who live for and by the Spirit are Children of God.[50] Understanding how to do this becomes the spiritual journey every believer is called to walk. We will talk later in the book about the tension between the physical and spiritual locus of control. Becoming free from the law of death is a conscious effort of giving control to the Holy Spirit. Taking the control away from the natural tendency of human control is simple to understand but sometimes is very difficult to do. The appetites of the natural body scream for the soul's attention. The human body must be taught that it is not in control. This struggle is part of spiritual formation, and it is important in becoming full of God's love. The achievement of victory in this struggle leads to finding inner strength and health.

According to Francis Chan,

In the craziness of our world, it takes tremendous effort to find a quiet place. It takes time to quiet your mind and your heart before the Lord. It means turning off the music, the television, or your cell phone. It might mean going outside to your favorite spot. For some, this is curling up inside in the only place where you find privacy. For others, it might mean heading to whatever wilderness is nearest to you or booking a few days at a local retreat center.[51]

Finding time to be with the Holy Spirit and making Him a priority takes a tremendous amount of discipline. Few Christians find the right mix of stopping and waiting on God in the daily hurry of Western life. As a pastor, I find this true in my life also. "Doing God's work," in and of itself can become a distraction to the intimacy the Lord calls all of us to experience.

A church can bustle with activity and energy, which can appear to be life-giving; however, if the Holy Spirit is not doing the moving, the church will soon find itself without the real power needed to bring glory to God. The excesses from the past in the manifestations of the Holy Spirit should not be allowed to swing the pendulum toward the extreme reaction of despising the Spirit's moving. The leadership of each church needs to take a hard look at the true spiritual life of the church as well as their intimacy level with the Father. He has called us to a wonderful life—full and rewarding.

LDP = PLDP + SLDP

God created life to operate according to His design. To fulfill the Gospel mandate upon the Church, each believer must function according to that design. It then is important to explore, what I call, Life Design Protocols (LDP). These etiquettes have the potential to be followed or violated each day. God created this planet with these protocols; however, post fall of man, they have been disrupted. These LDP violations have caused much damage in both the physical and spiritual realm. The Church must consider these designs as She determines to take the Gospel forward. One of the major plays by the Enemy, that thwarts the aggressive advancement of the Gospel in the Earth is by bringing death, resistance, and destruction through LDP violation.

LDP consists of two separate but parallel design energies. I will divide them into two groups for the sake of clarity. It is important to remember that though they seem to be two distinct areas of life, they are interactive reciprocally. The first, more obvious of the two, I term, Physical Life Design Protocols (PLDP). God commanded this world into existence from nothing. He created all that is physical; He set it into motion by design. The universe has physicality. The world has dimension, time, and space. The physical reality operates upon the governing laws of God's design and plans. He is not locked into our time and space. However, we live in Him, move, and have our being. Our experience in this life operates best when the PLDP and the second set of designs (SLDP) are followed.

Abundant life is only possible if the Spiritual Life Design Protocols (SLDP) are maximized. The SLDP connect our existence to infinity and gives the follower everything needed for life and godliness. Our lives are hidden with Christ. We were slain in Christ before the foundation of the world.[52] The Bible also teaches that we are now seated and connected with Jesus in the heavenlies.[53] It is not my intention to explain the full implication for these eternal realities but to give a theological frame of reference point. The takeaway at this point is, there is a very real spirit-realm that we are connected to and can move into God's SLDP. The best picture of the amalgamation of the two subcategories of LDP can be seen in the life of Jesus. According to the Holy Scriptures, Jesus is fully God and fully man. Jesus incarnated the Godhead, making known the nature of God to the physical creation.

> Abundant life is only possible if the Spiritual Life Design Protocols (SLDP) are maximized.

As followers of Jesus, it is our responsibility to walk this journey of life and use it to advance His Gospel to the ends of the earth. It becomes more than just living a long life; it is taking the full advantage of being the temple of the Holy Spirit to make the name of Jesus spectacular and far-reaching. The challenges ahead of the Church today will require a tremendous amount of grace empowerment and cooperation with the Holy Spirit. Worldwide darkness and deception position itself to mislead, if possible, the elect of God.[54] The followers in today's Church must be ready to fight the good fight. The enemy of our soul will do whatever is necessary to distract, disable, detour, and discourage the Church's advancement. He will use all forms of deception to get us to throw off our confidence. The believer must cooperate with God's design to become strong physically, mentally, emotionally, and spiritually. Following God's protocols for life will allow His people the resiliency needed to finish well.

Throughout the book, we will look at each LDP as they apply to the things we can control by cooperating with the designs of God's universe. Below is a list of the protocols that will be unpacked in detail. Remember, although I have separated these into two subcategories, the interactional effects are parallel. Every follower must incarnate the Word of God in their lives, and this makes every aspect of life spiritually connected to infinity. The message here is not just healthy spiritual growth that allows for effectual ministry, but it includes the sustainability of Gospel advancement.

> The message here is not just healthy spiritual growth that allows for effectual ministry, but it includes the sustainability of Gospel advancement.

LDP

PLDP	SLDP
Bodily Discipline	Self-reductionism[‡]
Marginal Management	Sabbath[§]
Restorative Sleep	Solitude
Nutrigenomics[*]	Meditation
IPNB[†]	Connectivity
Hydration	Contemplation
Environmental Exposure	Munificence[**]

---

[*] *The study of the interaction of nutrition and genetics.*
[†] *IPNB stands for Interpersonal Neurobiology (first developed by Dan Siegel and Allan Schore) the primary theory and practical working model which describes human development and function as being a product of the relationship between body, mind and relationships. It includes but is not limited to the effects of social-genomics (effects of relationships on genetics).*
[‡] *Self-reductionism is used here in the context of willfully reducing self in light of promoting spiritual growth (spiritual reduction of self which allows healthy growth in the inner man).*
[§] *Sabbath is the spiritual discipline of restorative weekly connection to God by His Spirit and the reality that Christ has finished the work of redemption and given His followers the power of life change that works every day.*
[**] *Munificence used here as a spiritual discipline of God-like generosity.*

Every person struggles with one or more areas of design. The vital thing to remember is to struggle in them, not with them. These fourteen areas are not something extra to add to one's life; these fourteen areas are the very life-determinates to how well we connect to family, others, and God. The better these protocols are operating results in effectiveness, longevity, and generational ability to advance the kingdom of God in the Earth. It's important to operate in the knowledge that believers already are overcomers because of a faith position.[55] It then becomes the faith action to move within the design of God, allowing the Holy Spirit to do the sanctifying work of producing His fruit through followers. The church must equip the body to fulfill the work of ministry. Equipping becomes more than just motivational; it becomes transformational. This power is only released by, and through, the Holy Spirit into the assembly. Leadership's role is to watch over the flock pointing toward Jesus and removing anything that would grieve God's Spirit. The Church of Jesus is designed to be a fellowship of encouragement, edification, correction, connection, and unity. This integrated unity is achieved through the knowledge of Jesus and His teachings.

The purpose of this book is to reinforce the idea that church growth that lasts must be healthy. Health is multifaceted and interconnected, as well as amalgamated into all the LDP. Jesus is building a Church that is unstoppable. This radical Church remains effective only as She remains healthy. The decisions, direction, and commitment of today will determine the lasting power well into the following generations. The success and problems of tomorrow's Church are being lived out now. Building alongside Jesus is a walk of healthy faith. Whatever He builds will last, and the gates of Hell will not stand in the way. The current health crisis in America is a reminder of how poor health impedes every area of life. Followers that are taken out of the fight due to unnecessary physical, emotional and spiritual issues has circumvented the movement of the Church in America and appears to be an exponential problem. Too many churches have begun well but have become sick and unproductive because the LDP were violated in some fashion, and their failure to bring the needed prescription for correction and healing has not been realized. It's time for followers to embrace their calling and be their best for the long hall. The world is waiting and will be transformed as the Church of Jesus grows into Her destiny by His strength and vigor. The world needs the Church, and the Church has something great to offer.

3.2 CREATED FOR CONNECTION: THE RELATIONAL FACTOR

We are created for a connection to God that draws others into relationship with Him. In the story of the Garden of Eden, as God created humanity, His intention of being known to His creation becomes evident. The relational connection between two individuals is also displayed as God makes Adam and Eve. God states that it is *not good for man to be alone* (unconnected).[56] At Adam's first reaction to the introduction of his new wife, he says, *This is now bone of my bones, and flesh of my flesh; she shall be called Woman because she was taken out of Man.*[57] It is apparent from the Genesis story that God would directly connect to His new creatures, and the creatures were designed to connect. When the federal head of mankind (Adam) chose to disconnect from God, physical, emotional, mental, and spiritual death resulted. Sin and lies perverted the very image of God that was given to mankind. This disconnection of humanity from God and others created a world of distortion in God's designed purpose and function for relationships.

God created us for connection to Himself and others. Humanity, in its pre-fallen state, was wired to connect with God. The story of the fall of man is the story of disconnection from God and separation, with isolation, from others. God so desired to be reconnected with His creation that He took the offense upon Himself and paid the total price for the reconnection. As Jesus died on the cross, He paid for the reconnection of mankind. As the Gospel goes forward, those who turn from living for self and reattach to the life-giving Spirit become His offspring. When sin entered the world, humanity truly died because of this separation. It is the very heart of God to bring many sons to glory and thus to undo the death brought on by the fall. Man rejected God and must receive His offer to become reunited through the costly blood of Jesus.

Recorded in the Scripture is a secret of the foundational make-up of the human soul. *He has made everything appropriate in its time. He has also set eternity in their heart, yet so that man will not find out the work which God has done from the beginning even to the end.*[58] Down deep in the essence of every human being is the "knowing" that there is infinity.

> *That they would seek God, if perhaps they might grope for Him and find Him, though He is not far from each one of us; for in Him we live and move and exist, as even some of your own poets have said, "For we also are His children." Being then the children of God, we ought not to think that the Divine Nature is like gold or silver or stone, an image formed by the art and thought of man.*[59]

The physical body responds to this notion and self-regulates in relationship to this reality. The Laws of Thermodynamics are acted upon by the psychological nature of the human systems. Even at the sub-cellular level, the inner workings of our design combat the First Law of Thermodynamics.[*] The Second Law of Thermodynamics is seen in the brain systems and regulates life accordingly. It is as if the human body knows where it came from and where it is going—infinity. According to Glenn G. Dudley, MD, "God has necessarily been encoded in neural design as well as in the body image in order that infinity anticipation and the restraint of the Second Law by an image can have neural relevance."[60]

---

[*] *The first law of thermodynamics is a version of the law of conservation of energy, adapted for thermodynamic systems. The law of conservation of energy states that the total energy of an isolated system is constant; energy can be transformed from one form to another but can be neither created nor destroyed.*

The brains regulatory systems of ponderostatic[*] and thermoregulatory[†] functions are linked to the preconceived notion of eternity. These systems did not evolve over a period of time but must, by their very nature exist simultaneously in a moment for life to exist.

Again, Dudley states,

We will see that clarification comes from understanding an image as a probabilistic, if-then event connected to the fundamental mechanisms of energy regulation. We surmise that in a person the overseeing self actually *is* the interface between the past and the future—and, equivalently, between order and disorder, respectively. Linked to the thermodynamics of matter in this way, we concluded that the self has adequacy or 'dimension' that is inseparable from the energy-regulating core of the brain as it functions reciprocally with three-dimensional, somatotopic[‡] organization of the cerebral cortex[§] just proximal to the limbic brain[**] in which the nuclei for energy regulation are found.[61]

Said simply, there appears to be a physical link, and hard wiring of the brain, as it relates to the idea that it is finite and will at some point return to the original state of weightlessness (nonphysical existence) and reacts to this reality. The negentropic[††] nature of human structures and existence is the miracle of God called "life." One way we are made

---

[*] *Ponderostatic is the brain's functional system purposed for weight regulation.*

[†] *Thermoregulatory is the brain's functional system purposed for heat regulation of the body.*

[‡] *Somatotopic is the relating to or mediating the relation between particular body parts and corresponding motor areas of the brain.*

[§] *Cerebral cortex is the outer layer of the cerebrum composed of folded gray matter and playing an important role in consciousness.*

[**] *Limbic brain is involved in motivation, emotion, learning, and memory. The limbic system is where the subcortical structures meet the cerebral cortex.*

[††] *Negentropic is life's ability to reduce entropy (and corresponding increase in order). Life has the ability to take food (dead material) for instance and apply forces to it to produce energy towards order.*

> The negentropic nature of human structures and existence is the miracle of God called "life."

in the image of God is by taking things of less order and making things of greater order. As the universe tends toward disorder (think of the dust under your bed), we are involved in creating order.

God has put eternity in our hearts. As we will see later in the book, the human heart has reasoning capabilities separate and parallel to that of the brain. The heart is connected to others by strong bonds and can "override" the normal brain's mode of operation. The conscience reality of the heart may cause many issues due to its intuitive nature. The Bible says it is desperately deceived and can operate outside of logical reason. The good news is that the heart is a very productive energy for connection and health. The human heart, if under the subjection of the Holy Spirit, has supernatural abilities as well as knowledge and connection to God. Later, in chapter 6 we will look more fully into this astounding ability of the heart to connect to God, others, and to change life outcomes. The heart is much more than a pump. The Bible teaches us to *Watch over your heart with all diligence, for from it flow the springs of life.*[62] The heart interconnection with the rest of the body may hold an important key that transcends the individual's life and can even reach into future generations. This heart connection is relational but also can change DNA tags, turning them on and off (methylation) and modify or modulate histones.[*] Simply stated, the heart is more than a pump, it is a connection point for relationships. The heart is so sensitive to relational connections that if it believes or perceives that relational events surpass the emotional pain threshold, it can shut the entire body down, which can lead to physical death.[†]

---

[*] *Histones are the chief primary proteins of chromatin, which DNA winds acting as spools. They control gene regulation.*
[†] *Takotsubo cardiomyopathy – cardiogenic shock due to loss or extreme emotional situation which can lead to death if not treated right away.*

Christian neuro-scientists have also discovered, through neurobio-logical* research, that the brain is wired for God. The latest studies have pointed to the fact that we were made to connect with God and others. Without this attachment, the brain becomes unhealthy and leads to further destructive consequences. According to Curt Thompson, M.D.:

Parents who are mindful of their children's needs and flexible in their interactions with them are literally assisting the neural wiring process in their children's brains. This enables their children to be open and receptive to the image of a God who is interested and delighted in them, compassionate and full of grace when they stumble, yet willing to discipline them without simul-taneously shaming. As they grow older, when life feels less integrated, more disconnected--when they want juice but are offered only milk; when they have a fight with their mom over the environmental disaster area they call their bedroom; when they develop cancer, they will still retain in their neural circuitry the imprint of a God who is there. A God of bone and blood. A God of strength, mercy, and mystery. A God of history, acting in their lives, the proof being in what they feel in a manner that is undeniable, rooted in their very bodies. And they do not simply have an awareness of this being 'true' as a fact (an explicitly encoded, dominantly left hemisphere function), but rather as an existential, emotional, remembering experience as a recalled auto-biographical memory (one that requires the integration of the left and right, as well as lower and higher regions of the brain.)[63]

COMMUNION

For the follower of Jesus, being "made alive" or "born again" means more than just a new destination after death. The new creature that has

---

Neurobiology is the biology of the nervous system.

been born from above has the spiritual capacity to commune with God through the power of the Holy Spirit. This reconnection and communion bring with it the power of life change. Jesus uses the analogy of the vine to demonstrate this reconnection and states that apart from this attachment; followers can do nothing. The wiring is there; however, it will not be connected until it is surrendered to God. In Romans, it states;

> *For the wrath of God is revealed from heaven against all ungodliness and unrighteousness of men, who suppress the truth in unrighteousness, because that which is known about God is evident within them; for God made it evident to them. For since the creation of the world His invisible attributes, his eternal power and divine nature, have been clearly seen, being understood through what has been made, so that they are without excuse.*[64]

The thriving church then should be a place where people are not only accepted into the group but given the Gospel of reconnection. This evangelistic message is good news indeed! The Gospel is the invite to the restored relationship of mankind with the Creator. Healthy church growth happens in a place that administers reconciliation and reconnection.

The healthy church functions as a "body." The Gospel calls out to all. The ones that turn from their independence to dependence upon God, He places into interdependent relationships with other followers. This group then is in total reliance upon the Holy Spirit's guidance and direction. The individual parts rely on Him to function together as a group. All the parts are necessary for the overall healthy spiritual growth of the church. This interconnectivity, when operating in unity, causes the body to grow in a way that looks and behaves more and more like the Master.

The science of Interpersonal Neurobiology has much to show us about the relationship and interactions of people with people. The relationships of healthy spiritual individuals within the Body of Christ and the effects of their health to the larger group is important to be understood if the church is to experience healthy growth. The author of *What Your Body Knows About God*, Rob Moll, states;

Our connection to other people begins at birth. At the end of pregnancy, mothers' oxytocin receptors spike in their brains. This chemical is a "feel good" chemical of the brain, and it assists in social bonding: the female brain is preparing itself to experience extra joy and love as the mother bonds with her new baby. At the same time, babies are ready to connect to their mothers. Studies have found that when shown pictures of faces, infants just ten minutes old will look at them longer than similar patterns that are not faces. 'A newborn's brain expects faces,' says neuroscientist David Eagleman.[65]

Again, Curt Thompson says:

The neuroscience is clear: the concept of a single functioning neuron or a single functioning brain simply does not exist in nature. Without input from other neurons, a single neuron will die. Likewise, without input from other minds, a single mind becomes anxious, then depressed, then hopeless, and then dies, either by intentional means (suicide) or more passive forms of poor self-care. It is not good for a man or woman-or a neuron or a brain-to be alone.[66]

Our Western culture values independence, self-reliance, and individualism. The lack of the concept of being needed, affected, necessary, and interdependent upon a group may be one of the main hindrances to healthy church development. This culturally driven value must be addressed with Biblical insight and instruction. The hand cannot cut itself off from the rest of the body if the group's spiritual life is to happen. The implications of this truth have overreaching consequences. Each person has a responsibility to the group to be the best they can be

> Each person has a responsibility to the group to be the best they can be in their own spiritual life for themselves and others.

in their own spiritual life for themselves and others. In the following sections, we will consider how Spiritual Life Design Protocols (SLDP) encourage the soul of the individuals toward healthy spiritual living which will benefit and flourish the church.

Connection first begins with individual integration. For instance, the physicality over-emphasis of our society and its obsession with the body's appearance to the exclusion of mental, spiritual, and emotional wellbeing, becomes an unhealthy dynamic. Focusing exclusively on emotional stability alone will lead to self-absorption. Without a holistic, integrated approach to existence, it is certain that this imbalance will lead to disintegration in one form or another. Likewise, a church that addresses only the spiritual needs of a congregation will not be healthy. Jesus most often met the felt or practical needs of the people before He applied the spiritual solution. It is important for the amalgamation of heart, mind, soul, and body in an integrated fashion for the expression of God's design to be fully realized. This interwoven nature of the different human experiences leads to a human expression relatable to all. For the healthy church to reach the culture, it is necessary to speak the cultural "language" of its felt needs. Healthy integrated individuals make up the potential for the Body of Christ that can expand its influence beyond the religious few.

In discipleship, the understanding of the interactive effects of body, soul, and spirit by the leader is necessary to help the disciple grow into all aspects unto Christ. Christian counseling must be viewed as intentional, intense discipleship. When counseling, all areas of human existence should be taken under consideration. The relegation of the counselee's problems exclusively to a spiritual issue is incomplete. Many times, in my practice, I have discovered grave medical conditions that were not the result of faulty belief constructs. Hormonal imbalance, grief, biochemical deficits, or failure in critical Physical Life Design

Protocols (PLDP) were the cause—not sin. Understanding human integration of body, soul, and spirit becomes key for the spiritual health of people and the church.

BODILY DISCIPLINE

"Bodily discipline is only of little profit, but godliness is profitable for all things, since it holds promise for the present life and also for the life to come"
1 Timothy 4:8

It is clear from this passage that SLDP are eternally significant. The effect of the SLDP brings with them the benefit in both realms. Admittedly, if the choice had to be made between spiritual growth and physical training, the spirit's life would take priority. After all, the body is the temple of the Holy Spirit, and the new creature that has been made alive through regeneration is the goal of the Gospel. What this verse is *not* saying is that taking care of the temple has no value. The realization that in Heaven there is no temple, for God, Himself is the Temple[67] is fundamental. Until that day; the physical

> Proclaiming the Gospel through a person's daily activities is the incarnational aspect of the Christian life.

earthly body is needed to move the Gospel to the ends of the Earth and communicate the love of God to the dying world. Proclaiming the Gospel through a person's daily activities is the incarnational aspect of the Christian life. We are commanded to care for our temple and build the kingdom on Earth until we exit.

According to the grace of God which was given to me, like a wise master builder I laid a foundation, and another is building on it. But each man must be careful how he builds on it. For no man can lay a foundation other than the one which is laid, which is Jesus Christ. Now if any man builds on the foundation with gold, silver, precious stones, wood, hay, straw, each man's work will become evident; for the day will show it because it is to be revealed with fire, and the fire itself will test the quality of each man's work. If any man's work which he has built on it remains, he will receive a reward. If any man's work is burned up, he will suffer loss; but he himself will be saved, yet so as through fire. Do you not know that you are a temple of God and that the Spirit of God dwells in you? If any man destroys the temple of God, God will destroy him, for the temple of God is holy, and that is what you are.[68]

We are to steward everything under our responsibility and to keep ourselves available, so we can be about God's work. He calls us to the holiest duty of loving Him with all our hearts, minds, souls, and strengths. The strength speaks of our physicality. I think this need for physical readiness is greatly overlooked. This greatest of all the commands is our highest aim. And, it includes the total unification of the follower's experience. Likewise, the great commission of Christ to His followers is to, *Go therefore and make disciples of all the nations, baptizing them in the Name of the Father and the Son and the Holy Spirit, teaching them to observe all that I commanded you; and lo, I am with you always, even to the end of the age.*[69]

I don't know if you have ever thought about how physically challenging this commandment is. What does it take to complete this task? What type of issues stalls or completely circumvent these instructions? The pendulum of bodily physical importance tends to swing in one of two directions. It swings between neglect (sometimes damage) and self-absorption. Our Western culture makes much of the physical appearance of self and celebrates the beauty of a well-sculptured body. There is money to be made by potential diets and workout plans that promise results by giving a person their dream body. It is no wonder some churches downplay body focus. The landing spot for the balance of good health is such that it allows the individual the longevity and strength to complete the heavenly assignment. The real-time problem of our day, physical health and its care, is evident. I believe one of the enemy's greatest tools used against the Church today is self-indulgence, which keeps Her sick and unable to move when God calls. Satan does this by deceiving. Satan uses lies about our state of physical health and infers the idea that, as we get older we are supposed to get sick. These thoughts need to be made captive and brought to Christ.

Bodily discipline is a multifaceted subject. The subject includes many interactions with the SLDP. The primary focus at this point in the book, however, will be in the realm of physical exercise. There are many factors to consider when applying this subject to the individual. A person's history, age, physical health, DNA makeup, and vocation all play important roles in holistic health. The goal here is to remember that the purpose and end state of physical health is remaining available to God and His calling. Looking for a habit that best fits the person and his/her situation is critical. The goal of physical training is to help the body function properly for longevity. Knowing and understanding your BMI, blood pressure, heart rate, and body condition should be the starting point. It is important to "know your numbers." The other consideration that parallels physical training is nutrition and nutrigenomics (which will be discussed later in the book).

In some cases, the primary care physician should be consulted before starting any radical physical training. God has called all His followers to steward their physical bodies with care. It wasn't until I turned 60 that I realized this important aspect of life. I hope that some will heed this instruction and become usable to God's purposes for the duration of their lives. I think it is never too late to reverse damage caused by past violations of the LDP.

I was challenged by the Holy Spirit to take the shape of my body seriously. My body had seen abuse for years, and I was terribly out of shape. I was headed down a path I thought was just the path everyone takes. I had lost my dad, mom, older brother, and my sister. My younger brother (the only immediate parental family member I have left) was struggling with a traumatic brain injury and was recovering from major brain surgery. I realized that if I was going to finish well and fulfill the call on my life, I needed to take my physical health seriously. All my life I loved cookies, cake, and candies. I ate whatever I wanted. I had become obese and had high blood pressure, kidney issues, blood infections, high cholesterol, neurological abnormalities, and struggling with cognition. I was the Senior Pastor of RockFish Church with unrelenting stress. I believe the Lord spoke to me, that if I did not change the way I was headed, I would not be around much longer. I always thought that I would die young. I just gave into the natural plan of all senior adults. I believed the lie! You know, overweight, high blood pleasure, have an open-heart procedure to keep you going, get diabetes, lose a kidney or two, go on dialysis (which both my brother and father faced and died from) and maybe have a stroke. My sister died at 55 from cancer that spread to the brain, and my older brother died at 60. Please hear me! This lie is not God's plan! He wants to have you finish well. Some sicknesses come no matter how well you take care of yourself, but do your part treasuring the gift God has given you.

By God's grace, the story did not end there. I am now 64, 70 pounds lighter, run at least three times a week (5-8 miles), workout, off all my medicine, my blood pleasure is normal, cholesterol is 160 (total), triglycerides 73 and I have a tremendous amount of energy to give the kingdom. My heart is to finish well, doing my best to take care of this wonderful gift called life. My goal is not to live longer to retire and see the world; it is to advance God's kingdom as long as I can--forcefully. RockFish church is currently involved in reaching, training, equipping, and supporting the broken families and orphans in the Middle East. This type of outreach takes a reserve of mind, body, and soul. The challenges are great, but we serve the powerful God who spoke this all into existence. He has everything needed for life and God-likeness, and He has designed us to complete our tasks.

Physical health helps all aspects of life. The brain thrives on oxygen and blood flow. Raising the heart rate and stressing the body in a good way helps: mood, digestion, restorative sleep, relationships, eliminate toxins, aid in physical, mental, and emotional energy; telomere resiliency,* epigenetic† enhancement, and reduce emotional stress. It assists in clearing up foggy thinking and increases mental reserve. Working out forces the re-prioritizing of time allocation which helps with marginal management (one of the other important PLDP). Physical activity helps increase testosterone which assists with many health benefits, especially for men. Although the bodily discipline of the physical nature is not effective, in and of itself, it is a critical component to physical longevity and resiliency. God created this incredible body that can endure a lot, and if treated as designed, can take the believer to the end of a well-run race. God has given us all a race to run, and it will not be completed if we don't finish well.

> God created this incredible body that can endure a lot, and if treated as designed, can take the believer to the end of a well-run race.

MARGINAL MANAGEMENT

"Which one of you by being anxious can add a single cubit to his life's span?"
Matthew 6:27

Marginal management is a decision-making tool that helps prioritize LDP that maximizes kingdom potential. It is put under the PLDP subcategory because it begins in the physical realm, even though it touches all areas of life. Besides creating the needed space for kingdom advancement, it allows for stress management, resiliency, and reserves.

---

* *Telomere resiliency is the slowing of the rate of the biological aging process. Telomeres protect the ends of the DNA. They are protective sheaths of proteins that are used up during cell division.*
† *Epigenetics is the set of the alterations of genetic material that modifies gene expression. Genetic DNA tags are switched on or off, but don't alter the genes themselves. It also influences histone performance.*

Needed reserves of the brain, emotion, spirit, soul, and body are fundamental for the follower to complete the mission of Christ. The Christian life, if lived according to the scriptures is always a supernatural endeavor. The mastery of the management of time, priority, and intensity is a life-long journey. In Western culture, the pace is so relentless that the resources of time, opportunities, and money are marginless. Resource management is needed to get through each week. Adding one more activity or cost to the already stretched lifestyle seems impossible.

Disregarding the PLDP of Marginal Management has potentially grave consequences. I think the book *Margin,* written by Dr. Richard Swenson[70] should be read and applied by every follower of Jesus. Our culture is plagued with chronic fatigue, stress, worry, and fear. The damage of constant stress on the body is becoming manifested in an array of life debilitating conditions. Marginal Management, like the other LDP, is a biological imperative for the thriving of body, soul, and spirit. The triune* homeostatic† needs of the human must be considered for the holistic ability to function unimpeded. The physical body responds poorly to negative stress. It does not function in isolation from the soul and spirit. There is perpetual Reciprocal Cybernetic Inductional Interaction‡ (RCIIH) between the body and the soul and spirit. (In chapter 4, we will endeavor to map this separate but parallel effect of the interactions on the essence of a person). The integrated earthly body does not function in seclusion from the soul and spirit and vice versa. When there is stress, the consequences are much more than just psychological, physiological, spiritual or emotional. Negative stress reaches into the realm of the Interpersonal Neural Biology between self and others. For instance, the process of neuroception can trigger a fear response outside of a logical reason, but social interaction or feedback

---

* *Consisting of three in one (body, soul, spirit in this context).*
† *The tendency toward a relatively stable equilibrium between interdependent elements, especially as maintained by physiological processes.*
‡ *Reciprocal Cybernetic Inductional Interaction is the hypothesis of the separate but parallel waves of influence between systems of the body, soul and spirit without physical contact.*

can down-regulate the fear and stress response as it activates the sympathetic nervous system. According to Dr. Steven Porges,

> Neuroception is not a cognitive process; it is a neural process without a dependency on awareness. Neuroception is dependent on a neural circuit that evaluates risk in the environment from a variety of cues and triggers shifts in autonomic state to adaptively deal with the cues.[71]

Understanding the need for margin building in every area of life becomes a high priority that builds resiliency and longevity. This ability to create life margin serves the Kingdom purposes well. Creating margin reduces stress and brings protection against many negative health issues. Dealing with stress reduces financial, medical, time, relational, and vocational burdens. Stress has been linked to a myriad of physical, emotional, and spiritual immobilizations. It is difficult to pick up a book or article on modern medical abnormalities without finding some form of linkage to stress. These effects are long-standing and, in some cases, transgenerational.[*] Stress has been linked to everything from in utero source of adult-onset mood disorders to Alzheimer's. Stress has been shown to cause DNA epigenetic expression related to cancer and other major issues due to stress-induced methylation[†] of the DNA and histone[‡] modulation. One example was presented by Dr. Nessa Carey, a geneticist with a Ph.D. in Immunology, and author of The Epigenetics Revolution. She writes,

> Stress has been linked to everything from in utero source of adult-onset mood disorders to Alzheimer's.

---

[*] *Transgenerational effects of stress have been demonstrated in many studies indicating dramatic results of stress across generations.*
[†] *Methylation can change the "on and off" switching tags that changes the DNA expressional activity without changing the sequence.*
[‡] *Histones are proteins that package and order the DNA into structural formations which help regulate genes and expression.*

Even more extraordinary, some of these effects seem to be present in the children of this group, i.e., in the grandchildren of women who were malnourished during the first three months of their pregnancy. So, something that happened in one pregnant population affected their children's children. Not only in stress induced by poor nutrition, but traumatic childhoods that were abusive. But we know that adults who suffered traumatic childhoods are actually over-stressed. They produce too much cortisol, all the time. Something must be going wrong in this feedback loop. There are a few studies in humans that show that this is the case. These studies examined the levels of the corticotrophin-releasing hormone in the fluid bathing the brain and spinal cord. As predicted, the levels of the corticotrophin-releasing hormone were higher in individuals who had suffered childhood abuse than in individuals who hadn't.[72]

According to Doctor Stephen Porges;

> Polyvagal Theory emphasizes that danger and life threat elicit different defensive response profiles. According to the theory, danger reactions are associated with the accepted notions of a stress response expressed in increases in autonomic activation through the sympathetic nervous system[*] and the adrenals. However, Polyvagal Theory also identifies a second defense system related to life threat that is characterized by a massive down-regulation of automatic function by an ancient pathway of the parasympathetic nervous system.[†] We are all familiar with the negative effects of the "classic" stress response,

[*] *Sympathetic Nervous System in response to danger reacts to increased blood flow throughout the body to support fight/flight behaviors.*
[†] *Parasympathetic Nervous System responds to support homeostasis, health, growth, and restoration. It also has the capacity to shutdown life functions.*

which interferes with the health-supporting functions of our nervous system. By disrupting the regulation of autonomic, immune, and endocrine systems, stress creates vulnerability for both mental and physical illnesses. However, missing from these discussions is a description of a second defense system with a feature not of mobilization as manifested in fight/flight reactions, but of immobilization, behavioral shutdown, and dissociation. Although fight/flight behaviors are functionally adaptive in response to danger cues, fight/flight behaviors are less adaptive when there is an inability to escape or physically defend. In contrast to fight/flight reactions, the response to life threat elicits a second defense system, which is expressed as immobilization and dissociation. When the body immobilizes in defense, it goes into a unique physiological state that is potentially lethal.[73]

What Dr. Porges is pointing out here is the idea that stressors have far-reaching effects beyond reactional adjustments. Much of the autonomic nature of the body's natural defense system is just that--autonomic. Our physical brain responds to all types of stress by automatic responses of the freeze, fight, flight, faint, or fail. The term "fail" used here to help define the Vagal Paradoxical Response[74] can include extreme protective measures that may precipitate long-term fainting, sinus arrhythmia,* bradycardia, defecation, and even death through shutting down the heart.

The failure to create marginal space has far-reaching implications. The follower has options and choices that should take in the realization that, for him, his life has been purchased for a purpose; this purpose is for the sons and daughters of God to be about His business proclaiming the Good News and making disciples of all nations. This process can be

---

* *Sinus arrhythmia: The normal increase in heart rate that occurs during inspiration (when breathing in quickly).*

stopped due to LDP being ignored or violated. Doctors Elizabeth Blackburn and Elissa Epel state that negative stress and poor life skill management can increase the biological aging process in dramatic ways.

> The ways you live can, in effect, tell your telomeres[*] to speed up the process of cellular aging. But it can also do the opposite. The foods you eat, your response to emotional challenges, the amount of exercise, whether you were exposed to childhood stress, and even the level of trust and safety in your neighborhood—all of these factors and more appear to influence your telomeres and can prevent premature aging at the cellular level.[75]

Creating space for the financial periphery, body (physical) backup, emotional resiliency, time availability, relationship capital building, spiritual connectivity, brain reserve, and general, restorative activities will determine the usefulness of believers in God's plan. To do this life, we must "show up" ready to be used for Jesus in our lives. The ability to steward, create, and manage our resources is a key PLDP. God has designed the way for this to happen most fruitfully. Following His design will help the Body of Christ to become all she was designed to become. The Enemy will try to stop us from following these LDP to impede the efficacy of the Gospel.

Stress is one of the most profound producers of life issues. Stress is a symptom of poor marginal management. The greatest inhibitors to the high quality of life are the influence of stress on the disintegration of body, soul, and spirit hemostasis. The separate, but parallel, cybernetic interaction nature of body, soul, and spirit determines the well-being and health of the entire essence of the person. As a reminder, the goal of this type of health is not purely for the longevity of life and its quality, but it has immediate and transgenerational implications for the

---

[*]*Telomeres are compound structures at the end of the chromosome. They deteriorate over time and can determine biological age.*

furtherance of the Gospel and God's Kingdom operation. One of the major directives of Transforming G.R.O.W.T.H. is simply creating a stewardship model that emphases availability of the Church and individuals for usefulness to the Gospel God.

> As a reminder, the goal of this type of health is not purely for the longevity of life and its quality, but it has immediate and transgenerational implications for the furtherance of the Gospel and God's Kingdom operation.

Integration of subcategories of this concept needs to be explored as well. The collapse of connections between man and God can result from the breakdown within the areas of the body, soul, or spirit. The body, for instance, needs sleep as well as good nutrition, good water, good air, low stress, and exercise. Any life health issue may lead to compounded and complex problems in other areas. Lack of the amalgamation of the soul due to shame, unconfessed sin, unbelief, or unforgiveness may have a devastating outcome on the connection to self, others and God. Mind dissonance due to problems in consciousness, memory, narrative, temporal reflection or cognition in general, leads to faulty emotional intelligent assessments. Transformational growth is needed to enjoy a connection with God and others fully. This type of growth is only made possible by yielding the total being to Jesus. "Bootstrap" Christianity will never produce the needed outcome. Self-effort, apart from the Holy Spirit's power, will only lead to further discouragement and defeat. The part of the follower is to "mind the things of the Spirit" and give into His promptings. This book is NOT a self-help book for longer life. It is a guide of encouragement toward the healthy growth of body, soul, and spirit to become available as a willing vessel to be mightily used of God. The fulness God has intended for the Church and the believer is best accomplished with strong, healthy, resilient followers having sharp minds and whole emotions. The walk of all believers is just that, a corporate walk where each carries his/her load and are ready to help when crushing circumstances emerge.[76]

Total integration or sanctification is empowered by yielding to the Holy Spirit. Christ purchased us, thus justifying us completely. The applied work of the cross made possible the indwelling of God's Holy Spirit. The Holy Spirit is functionally pragmatic in that He can form Jesus in the believer. According to Galatians 3:13, Jesus redeemed us from the curse of the Law so that we might receive the faith-blessing of Abraham. The Epistle of Galatians says that the reason He did this was *so that we might receive the promise of God's Holy Spirit*. Visualize this: the very Power that created the universe shares this existence with the follower—*daily*! He works in the believer as the body, soul, and spirit come into their proper designs. The Scripture declares, *Now may the God of peace Himself sanctify entirely; and may your spirit and soul and body be preserved complete, without blame at the coming of our Lord Jesus Christ.*[77] Throughout this book, the salient theme of holistic integration of body, soul, and spirit for spiritual health will become apparent.

3.3 CENTERED ON JESUS: THE INFLUENCE FACTOR

Jesus is the reason for everything: Jesus plus/minus nothing. Jesus is our source, our hope, our Redeemer, our life, our all. The church's health is solely dependent upon the life-giving blood of the Savior and His indwelling presence. Apart from Jesus, we are not able to do anything. The church meetings, budgeting, directing, hiring, structuring, counseling, and living must be all centered around Him. This concept sounds fundamental; however, it is easy to "move past" the basic notion of the Lordship of Jesus and lean upon man's innovation and capabilities.

Pointing to Jesus and making His name spectacular, is the mark of a healthy person as well as a healthy church. The vitality and influence of a body of believers are directly connected to their ability to lift Jesus up in all things. A life or a church that is built upon anything other than Jesus and His teaching will eventually collapse. In every life, and in every church, storms roll in, and the foundation will be tested. Any life not squarely built upon this Rock will end in devastation. It is important to do a self-check on each aspect of life, as well as the church, to see if any area is being built upon something other than Christ and His teachings. A person does not need a church to get to heaven, but the Church is God's design for communicating this great story. The Church is His expression used to proclaim, transform, and connect peoples, cultures, and societies to Himself. Whenever a church believes and acts as if it, in and of itself, is needed for salvation, error and control are at work.

> A person does not need a church to get to heaven, but the Church is God's design for communicating this great story.

Staying close to the cross in all teaching and preaching, as well as throughout the entire ministry, will ensure safe, healthy growth. Maintaining a need to "go deeper" in teaching beyond the Gospel, shows a grave lack in the understanding of the depth of the love of God found in the Gospel (Straying into theological instruction on how God does what He does lead to the church not doing what He commanded and commissioned Her to do). The Gospel is the power of God. The Good News is the call, the trigger, the sustaining force, and the delivering power we are all to proclaim. Understanding this centrality will help guide the leadership of the church and help keep Her from impotence. It is the Name of Jesus through His finished work, that allows a person or a church to be positioned to receive the Holy Spirit. Without this indwelling, there is no hope, no transformation, no life changes or direction into the future.

Jesus and His teachings should be the focal point of the Church's existence. Followers are exactly that: "followers." The teachings of Jesus demand that the believers follow and submit. The faith of the believer, absent of the outworking of Christ's teachings, is faith in the wrong thing. Picking and choosing to follow some of the instructions will lead to imbalance and spiritual anemia. Radical trusting in what Christ has given will release spiritual vitality. Healthy growth of the church, as well as the follower, is correlated directly to this principle. A truly vigorous church is made up of healthy followers.

The influence of the church is not diminished by holding firm to the teachings of Jesus; quite the opposite, taking a stand for His truths will allow for true, lasting, strong, growth. Jesus never made it easy to shadow Him. Jesus would, many times, make hard demands and set high standards for people. Jesus told followers that to follow Him could mean being homeless, without families, giving up all worldly wealth, persecution, and even death.[78] The great challenge of the post-modern cultural church is to hold to the truth of His Word while sharing His love to the dying.

Jesus promises;

Not everyone that says to Me, "Lord, Lord," will enter the kingdom of heaven; but he who does the will of My Father who is in heaven. Many will say to Me on that day, "Lord, did we not prophesy in Your name, and in Your name perform many miracles?" And then I will declare to them, "I never knew you; depart from Me, you who practice lawlessness." Therefore, everyone who hears these words of Mine, and acts upon them, may be compared to a wise man, who built his house upon the rock. And the rain descended, and the floods came, and the wind blew, and burst against that house; and yet it did not fall, for it had been founded upon the rock. And everyone who hears these words of Mine, and does not act upon them, will be like a foolish man, who built his house upon the sand. And the rain descended, and the floods came, and the winds blew, and burst against that house; and it fell, and great was its fall.[79]

The incorporation of the Name and teachings of Jesus throughout church life is critical. If the main message communicated by the church places an overemphasis on the man in the pulpit, then the reason for gathering the church will become corrupt. The church will eventually find itself in decline or no longer in the position to give the life-giving message. Jesus always made disciples that made disciples. He taught that the job of the minister was to administrate ministry. In the short three years of Christ's ministry, He demonstrated time and time again that the disciples were to watch Him, join Him, and ultimately do the ministry themselves. He said it was better if He went away! Some churches are blessed to have great pulpit ministers. But it is the job of that leader to raise up other great speakers and leaders. Seeing the pastor as the Moses that goes up to the mountain of God to get His word and bring it back down to the people is not only incorrect but will create an unwholesome, short-lived situation. All leaders need to help the disciples learn how to get hold of God for themselves, not becoming dependent exclusively on the leader's connection with God.

Not only should the leadership watch over the pulpit ministry, it needs to look at every area of the church to ensure there is no secular, behavioral modifications, or the use of heavy-handed control being expressed in any area; from the children's church to the youth group, to the outreach ministries. The "lifting up" of Jesus and His Gospel must remain central in all areas for the church to be spiritually healthy. The children and the youth will become very confused if they are not taught the Gospel all the way through their church life experience. There is a tendency to help the parents of the children by giving the children help in a behavioral change to ease tension at home. Children must learn to mind and behave by realizing that obedience to the Gospel is the power of and for submission. The youth in church often learn what not to do and the dangers of this world, to the exclusion of the life-transforming power of the Gospel.

The Gospel must be simply taught. The total reality of life in Christ, being lived out throughout the leadership, parents, staff, and influencers of the Body, insures health. Continuity between what is being said and lived out must be the norm. Falling in love with Jesus, in ever increasing degrees, demonstrates the true health of the church. Spiritual growth is

> Falling in love with Jesus, in ever increasing degrees, demonstrates the true health of the church.

measured by closeness to Jesus. Intimacy with Christ is the measure of spiritual health. It is manifested through surrender and dying to self. Reduction of self is the robust spiritual growth roadmap. Followers must decrease in all ways as they move toward Christ-likeness.

At the beginning of the early Church, it was clear that the relationship with Jesus was the driving reason for church expansion in her influence that reached into the known world. These world-changers were mostly unlearned men that operated from a deep relationship with Christ through the Holy Spirit. Today's church seems to be overly concerned with titles, degrees, and correct exegesis in favor of experiencing Jesus. Not to negate the importance of proper interpretation and handling of God's Word, but to know, apart from His abiding presence, is a step back towards Pharisaical behavior. True knowledge of Christ comes from His Word and is experienced in a personal relationship with Him. Church and personal growth thrive in the soil of complete devotion to Jesus.

The main thrust of this type of powerful church could easily be overlooked. If you go back and read this section again while looking for the believer's part, you may discover the two forces at work. 1) The inspiration of the Holy Spirit only accomplishes growth, and 2) the feeling of a unified "they" as a body moving together gains true power. Psalm 133 explains the great benefit of unity. It states that when brothers come together in unity, God *commands* a blessing! Where there is unity, God commands the threefold blessing of the Hebrew Sabbath year.[80] This blessing is the major favor of God's grace to get crops and seeds that would carry the people of God through an entire year of non-work and celebration. What favor of God! This Psalm proclaims the command of God on His people in unity that included anointing, prosperity, and a great harvest.

It is the authority of the Holy Spirit that empowers the people of God to impact the world through their unified spiritual potency. It is common in the Western culturally-influenced church to see the same disunity, individuality and "what's in it for me" mindset that pervades secular society. God has so designed the Body of Christ to function as the natural body. When the human body becomes disunified, the power for life is diminished. Unity comes best when followers reduce self and follow the Master. Unity happens around Jesus. As all parts work properly, joint maturity occurs.[81] The interaction of each part on the other parts is the causation for the building up of the Body of Christ. Few realize or rightly discern this body dynamic. The design of God for the Church that leads to lasting impact upon the culture happens through corporate spiritual maturity.

Realizing the reality of how people affect one another is critical for the leader of a church to understand. People working together and getting along is not just nice to have, it becomes a primary LDP. God has made us interdependent. The universe is built upon this design. Dysfunctional sickness ensues where there are relationships of independence and dependence. The larger Body of Christ is a mirror reflection of the way the human body works. When the individual systems of the human body become exclusively dependent or independent in relation to one another, the health of the body suffers. Likewise, the human body needs other people around it to function as designed. People need people to be complete. Total independence from others results in devastating outcomes. Similarly, people that are codependent-driven live in unhealthy relationships that lead to destruction. People are designed to work interdependently. So is the Body of Christ!

God designed the universe to operate with connective relational properties. This operation is seen in all aspects of the physical and spiritual realms. These connections run by influence and interaction of forces of energy throughout the interconnected systems. It is recorded in the Book of Genesis that God "worked" for six days. The classical formula of work done is: work done = force x distance. Power is expressed in the equation: power = work done / time is taken. The standard for measuring this is the joule. A joule is the unit of measure for energy. Energy is power. By this definition, when God spoke the amount of energy released to create the universe was beyond massive. This action

God designed the universe to operate with connective relational properties.

of "work" was a release of energy. Our universe was acted upon from the spirit realm by the Holy Spirit using pure energy. The Holy Spirit is known as the "Life Force of God" in the Hebrew. The term "Ruach" is the unseen force exemplified with the power of the wind. In the New Testament, one of the terms used for the Holy Spirit is "Dunamis," the root word we use for dynamite. The indwelling power of the Holy Spirit in each believer is the New Creature's, Life Force.

For He delivered us from the domain of darkness and transferred us to the kingdom of His Beloved Son, in whom we have redemption, the forgiveness of sins. And He is the image of the invisible God, the first-born of all creation. For by Him all things were created, both in the heavens and on earth, visible and invisible, whether thrones or dominions or rulers or authorities—all things have been created by Him and for Him. And He is before all things, and in Him, all things hold together.* He is also head of the body, the church; and He is the beginning, the first-born from the dead; so that He Himself might come to have first place in everything.[82]

Jesus is the Deliverer, Transferrer, Redeemer, Forgiver, Image of God, First-born, Creator of everything, Owner, Alpha, Sustainer, Head, and the First! Notice He holds it all together. We serve a powerful, amazing God. Jesus has given us so much. Everything needed for life and transformation has been provided for the follower of Jesus. Seeing God as ethereal, a being that is too delicate or fragile is not understanding the very nature of God. His design works with energy and certainty that does not change. He holds all things together by the *power* of *His Word*.

---

* *Emphasis added by author.*

God, after He spoke long ago to the fathers in the prophets in many portions and in many ways, in these last days has spoken to us in His Son, whom He appointed heir of all things, through whom also He made the world. And He is the radiance of His glory and the exact representation of His nature and upholds all things by the word of His power.[*][83]

In Chapter 4 we will look closely into the Spirit's power and energy for transformation. Seeing the interactional effects of energy in biological life is key to understanding the mind, body, soul and spirit interplay. Studies in Relational[†] and Interactive Biology[‡] confirm this interdependent unified design. This interdependent separate but parallel effects between body, soul, spirit and their systems are what I termed RCIIH.[§]

Influences concerning transformational growth is a broad matter. It is important to realize that the specificity of the SLDP found in the Bible is the Divine design solution for the dynamic forces altering the spiritual life.

Along with the PLDP, the congruent nature of the Cybernetic Inductional Interactional forces allows integration of the soul essence of the individual for optimal healthy growth. Simply put, "The Gospel God" has designed and given written instructions in His Word for the optimization of human experience that allows the believer to engage in God's global initiative of full redemption. Throughout this book, the interweaving of this concept will help clarify the purpose of the hierarchical nature of these influences. This concept can be cross-applied to the Body of Christ as well. Remember, the end state is cooperation with

---

[*] *Emphasis added by author.*
[†] *Relational Biology is a branch of mathematical biophysics relating to the connectiveness and biotopological nature of complex systems.*
[‡] *Interactive Biology looks at interactions of the environment, whole-organism biology including genetic, cellular, and morphological processes.*
[§] *Reciprocal Cybernetic Inductional Interaction Hypothesis is hypothesis of the separate but parallel waves of influence between systems of the body, soul and spirit without physical contact.*

God's design for the longevity and transgenerational effectiveness of God's Church to reach the world with His Good News. This Gospel calls and empowers people to repentance and to place their faith in Jesus Christ.

3.4 BONES: THE GOVERNMENTAL FACTOR

"Pray, then in this way: Our Father who art in heaven, Hallowed be Thy name. Thy kingdom come. Thy will be done, on earth as it is in heaven. Give us this day our daily bread. And forgive us our debts, as we also have forgiven our debtors. And do not lead us into temptation, but deliver us from evil. For Thine is the kingdom, and the power, and the glory, forever. Amen."
Matthew 6:9-14

Jesus instructed His followers to pray this way. Ever wondered why of all the things He could have included He chose this emphasis? It is all about vertical and horizontal relationships. Loving God and loving people is the ultimate goal. Loving goes back to the foremost commandment in Scripture. These two separate but parallel commandment principles must have tremendously important implications. It encompasses two realms; the realm of the spirit and the physical as it connects the two in a parallel fashion. Taking a closer look, it becomes evident that there are forces of influences that run upward, outward and inward. The view of God's holy nature and His Kingdom seems to be the foundations to the whole prayer; it begins with kingdom authority and ends with it. Sandwiched between God's power and authority are personal provision, interpersonal relational connectivity (with a warning against unforgiveness), and movement. Movement in that Jesus teaches us to ask that The Father would not "lead us" into temptation and that God would "deliver us" from evil. Without unpacking the doctrines of original sin, the sin nature and temptation, suffice to say, within the context of the preceding section of this Biblical chapter, Jesus was discussing how not to practice religion. In the greater context of movement away from temptation and evil, it becomes necessary to talk about influence.

In this instructive prayer of Jesus, He gives the directive to ask God to influence the follower away from temptation and evil. The Scripture is clear that God does not tempt anyone.

Let no one say when he is tempted, "I am being tempted by God"; for God cannot be tempted by evil, and He Himself does not tempt anyone. But each one is tempted when he is carried away and enticed by his own lust. Then when lust has conceived, it gives birth to sin; and when sin is accomplished, it brings death. [84]

The question is not, does God lead me into temptation, but asking Him to show us how to avoid the influencers that will take us the wrong direction. The Scriptures explain that moral failure happens because one is carried away by lust. This part of Christ's prayer then instructs us to pray that God will influence us away from our natural fleshly desires. Our hearts are filled with many desires, wants, and needs. The heart has a great capacity for deception and manipulation. The Bible teaches that the unregenerate heart is the most wicked thing on the planet. [85] It states that there is no logically induced cure for it; the only hope is regeneration—a heart transplant! But Jesus is talking to believers in this prayer. They have new hearts that have the power of the Holy Spirit. It seems that the issue then is in the area of sanctification. Sanctification is a process of the applied work of Christ. Followers are always a work in progress capable of being led by influences that need to be considered in prayer. So, what are these influencers? Apostle Paul stated that he had a problem doing what he wanted to do, and he did things he did not want to do. Paul called this his "body of death."

For we know that the Law is spiritual, but I am of flesh, sold into bondage to sin. For what I am doing, I do not understand; for I am not practicing what I would like to do, but I am doing the very thing I hate. But if I do the very thing I do not want to do, I agree with the Law, confessing that the Law is good. So now, no longer am I the one doing it, but sin which dwells in me. For I know that nothing good dwells in me, that is, in my flesh; for the willing is present in me, but the doing of the good is not. For the good that I want, I do not do, but I practice the very evil that I do not want. But if I am doing the very thing I do not want, I am no longer the one doing it, but sin which dwells in me. I find then the principle that evil is present in me, the one who wants to do good. For I joyfully concur with the law of God in the inner man, but I see a different law in the members of my body, waging war against the law of my mind and making me a prisoner of the law of sin which is in my members. Wretched man that I am! Who will set me free from the body of this death? Thanks be to God through Jesus Christ our Lord! So then, on the one hand, I myself with my mind am serving the law of God, but on the other, with my flesh the law of sin.[86]

After looking at God's design for healthy spiritual growth, several factors can lead a person into temptation. When Paul wrote this passage, he was no neophyte believer. He was not a man with a character flaw. He had been walking with God for many years. He wrote this toward the end of his ministry. On a side note, it is nice to know that even the guy who penned much of the New Testament struggled within himself with the same difficulties as all of us. Besides the inner difficulties that lead us into temptations, there are external factors. The interpersonal dynamics of negative relationships, bad entertainment and trusting in poor leadership all have the power to draw us away. The prayer of Jesus covers all of these in this simple sentence, "lead us not." Any influence that takes the believer toward temptation and evil is to be confronted. Picking godly friends and excusing oneself from negative influencers is a great way to escape from temptation. Following disciple-makers that are trustworthy is another. Leadership is influence. The Body of Christ needs godly leaders. Jesus says that we are not to be called leaders or teachers in and of our right. The only legitimate leader in the Church is merely pointing to *the Leader* and His teachings, not making a kingdom of his own. Leaders are *only* to be followed as they follow Christ. There is another emphasis found in the Lord's prayer. God lead us away from leaders we would choose because they would help us fulfill our desires.[87] Church government then becomes critical in following the Gospel God and His mandate to reach the world.

Just as bones give the human body structure, the governmental philosophy of a church gives structure to the Body of Christ. The ability of the church to move forward is directly related to how the authority and power are delivered to the people. The power of church government is often overlooked as the causality for sickness and level of health in a church. These power structures can vary widely from church to church. They may be set in longtime held tradi-

> The power of church government is often overlooked as the causality for sickness and level of health in a church.

tions. Governance that serves the people needs to be accomplished in such a way that abuse and over-control do not infect the church. The proper structure should result in unity and empowerment.

Behold how good and how pleasant it is for brothers to dwell together in unity! It is like the precious oil upon the head, coming down upon the beard, even Aaron's beard, coming down upon the edge of his robes. It is like the dew of Hermon, coming down upon the mountains of Zion; for there the Lord commanded the blessing-life forever.[88]

This Psalm beautifully exemplifies the blessing of unity among the brethren. The blessing described here is the sixth year "triple harvest blessing" given by God in preparation for the seventh-year jubilee, instructed by God to the Hebrew children in Leviticus 25. The Israelites needed to have a super crop to celebrate an entire year without working. Good leadership structure fosters unity and "commands" God's blessing on the church. In Chapter 7 we will explore in detail the "Theocratic Tapestry" that leads to a healthy church structure.

3.5 MINISTRY: THE PHILOSOPHICAL FACTOR

As I mentioned, in the story of the Wizard of Oz, people come to the great city for diverse reasons. Their values, expectations, and history determine their reason for "going to church." Philosophical assumptions determine their purpose for attending church. Church, as well as the individual's spiritual formative health, is influenced directly by these norms. It is the responsibility of the leadership to help shape and many times reshape these effects, moving people towards God's intended reasons.

It is the prevailing philosophical purpose that will shape church culture. The culture of a church will override any good strategy. Much of the cognitive dissonance[*] of the individual and the disunity of the church can be traced back to these faulty presuppositions. Matt Chandler remarked, "While strategy and structure are essential, culture trumps them both. If you have strategies and structures inconsistent with your culture, the culture will swallow them."[89]

> The culture of a church will override any good strategy.

All the mottos, innovations, mission statements, and meetings will not prevail against a culture or individual that has not incarnated the reason for going to church. From the vantage point of the Gospel mission, we find the reason for gathering and living. This vantage point must be the prevailing force that drives the believers. The demonstration of this aim needs to be taught and lived out by the influencers in the church. Keeping a spiritual eye open to any slight deviation in ministry philosophy is one of the highest priorities of church leadership. Works salvation, social justice (apart from the Gospel), hierarchical leadership

---

[*] *Cognitive Dissonance—the inconsistency of thoughts, values or beliefs within one's self.*

structures, entertainment, self-improvement, grandstanding, or any divergence from Jesus-centered, Gospel-driven, servant-leadership thinking needs to be taken seriously and addressed.

Underestimating the prevailing worldly thought among the people will lead to spiritual drifting and ultimately spiritual sickness within a church. It is important to incorporate sound Biblical teaching that emphasizes dying to self and the notion that lives are given to Christ to advance His cause. Jesus asked for followers, not visionaries. He has given us the vision, and it is our job to discover where we are to energize that vision. Each church holds a unique part of the Grand Story and must seek Jesus for His vision for that church. The individual as well must discover their part of the story. It is not the job of the church to write its own story with its values and expectations and visions. The unique vision of each church must spring from the Gospel vision.

The same is true for the individual's philosophy of life. Having a true understanding of the call of Jesus on the believer, and the cost involved in following Him is included in healthy spiritual growth. This type of philosophy gets into the nitty-gritty of daily life. The examination process of every true believer is an all-encompassing task. The philosophy of life question asks, "Is there meaning to my existence?" and if so, "what is the meaning for my life?" The Bible has much to say about these two questions; however, the ramifications clash radically with modern Western culture. The clash between the Bible and cultural norms is where unhealthy conflict may ensue. The SLDP will help remedy the conclusion and offer practical ways to make the needed changes.

When the body, soul, and spirit become conflicted, there may be grave fallouts. As we have discussed earlier, when homeostasis is disrupted, dangerous stress mechanisms operate. This type of stress causes confliction of the mind, emotional trauma, biologically induced inflammation, and limbic response-looping, creating increased anxiety and poor physical health. Philosophy of life issues may also be compounded because of family expectations and value difference dynamics. These family connections can be great influencers for confliction or a bounty of support and encouragement. A statement made by Rob Moll says, "Furthermore, it isn't what you believe theologically that influences your behavior, it is who you are connected to."[90] The people in your inner circle will have a profound effect on the acting out of your life philosophy. The true individual philosophy of life belief structures are the main determinants of the perception of safety, power, worth and hope. We directly influence those around us with our true-life outlook and beliefs. Likewise, others transmit physiological cues that may help or hinder our inner growth through neurobiological activation. Echoed here by Porges,

> The calming of physiological state promotes opportunities to create safe and trusting relationships, which in themselves expand opportunities to co-regulate behavioral and physiological state. This "circle" of regulation defines healthy relationships in which the relationship supports both mental and physical health. In this model, our bodily feelings (i.e., autonomic state) function as an intervening variable contributing to our reaction to others. When we are in a mobilized state characterized by sympathetic activation, we are "tuned" for defense and not for promoting cues of safety or for responding positively to cues of safety, However, when the autonomic state is regulated by ventral vagal pathways, our social engagement system coordinates cues of safety through voice and facial expression to down-regulate defense in ourselves and in others.[91]

The aspect of social engagement is an interactional effect between people based upon how they perceive life. These philosophies about life transfer can, through interpersonal neurobiological pathways, ramp up or calm down themselves and others. Behaviors are not based upon stated doctrines or creeds, but true belief structures. In the same way, the church's

> Behaviors are not based upon stated doctrines or creeds, but true belief structures.

philosophy of applied Scriptural truth directly impacts the body more so than stated beliefs. It is important for each church to be keenly aware of these underlying philosophies. Bad doctrine, wrong teaching, under or over emphasis of one truth to the exclusion of all truth and incorrect psychologies can all lead to unhealthy subtleties.

Wrestling with philosophical life purpose is part of a life-long exploration. The Scripture has a philosophy designed right in it. God has not left us without directions for living. He has given us all the tools to understand how to live this life, and when we lack insight, on how to apply His designs. He tells us to ask for the wisdom needed, and He will answer. As you will see later in the book, the LDP of the PLDP and SLDP *are not* the direct forces needed for life transformational growth; they are the riggings we have under our control that move us into position to receive the power needed to accomplish the Great Commission.

4

G. R. O. W. T. H. –
RESPONSE REPENTANCE

*N*ow when they heard this, they were pierced to the heart, and
said to Peter and the rest of the apostles, "Brethren, what
shall we do?" And Peter said to them, "Repent, and let each
of you be baptized in the name of Jesus Christ for the forgiveness of
your sins; and you shall receive the gift of the Holy Spirit. "For the
promise is for you and your children, and for all who are far off, as
many as the Lord our God shall call to Himself."
Acts 2:37-39

The Gospel calls to each person to reconnect to God. Repentance that
turns away from trusting self to trusting in Jesus is the very cornerstone
of this message. In the garden of Eden, this disconnection took place by
not trusting in God and turning to self for life and fulfillment. The result
was death to the body, soul, and spirit. The reconnection benefit is life
to the body, soul, and spirit. God's call is a call to recouple to life. Many
attempts to correct mankind's situation have been attempted by
shortcutting repentance-seeking-forgiveness but to no avail. The redemption of mankind happens solely through the finished work of Jesus
on the cross. The Holy Spirit applies the power of Christ's death, burial,
and resurrection to anyone that will turn to Him. The power of Christ is
the first essential step in church and individual health.

Repentance is a lifestyle, not just an event. The church must call
people to repentance. Without this, spiritual development doesn't begin.

We are all called to turn away from our ways and surrender to His. Each person is constantly being transformed. The sanctification process is body, soul, and spirit integration. *Now may the God of peace Himself sanctify you entirely; and may your spirit, soul, and body be preserved complete, without blame at the coming of our Lord Jesus Christ.*[92]

I term the first Spiritual Life Design Protocol (SLDP)--Self-reductionism. Self-reductionism goes beyond turning from sin and turning to God only one time. Repentance is included as a subcategory of Self-reductionism, along with fasting, and all forms of moderation. Self-reductionism is listed first for a good reason. Jesus calls His followers to make a life switch with Him. He takes our sins, and we receive His righteousness. Believers that are radically abandoned and given to the advancement of the Gospel allows the message to advance throughout the Earth. The follower has been freed from all things and allowed to use the amoral things of this world without condemnation. The idea of self-reductionism is to use freedom to better serve Christ and His mission of love in the Earth.

> The idea of self-reductionism is to use freedom to better serve Christ and His mission of love in the Earth.

Not making full use of everything allowed but asking the bigger question, "how I can best use my life to fulfill God's call to go into the world and make disciples?" All things are "ok," but not all things build the kingdom. Much of the modern Christian way of thinking is limited to following Jesus one or two days of the week and then asking Him to give a blessing on the rest of life. It is as if to ask Him to follow us around as we carry on living the American way of life, rather than following Him into His great adventure of Gospel advancement.

The Gospel God calls His people to repent and to turn away from their agenda and turn to His. Response repentance is an all-embracing life call that reaches into every facet of the believer's life and being. Dying to a life that serves anything other than God's purpose and His redemptive goal is the call of Jesus on His disciples. This call is not at all foreign to our designed purpose. When life is filled with the Holy

Spirit of the Life-giving God and engaged in working in full cooperation with His eternal plan, the peace that is beyond understanding permeates the body, soul, and spirit of the follower. Repentance is the first response toward this new life in Christ. It does not stop at initial salvation but becomes a way to live each day forward. The joy in finding life in death is resurrection power. As the believer incarnates His Word into real-time, this power becomes a life of abiding in Him—the Vine of life. Jesus came to save souls, and this is the co-assignment of every Christian. The ability to incarnate this reality becomes hope for this world. A church filled with followers who have followed Christ into this "cross-life" will become a vehicle for radical kingdom advancement.

4.1 HEALTHY SOUL

Throughout the Bible, the driving commandment for humanity is to love God with every part of its being and to love others as themselves. This command is impossible to fulfill in the dead fallen state of an unregenerate soul. The new birth is the reconnection with God through obedience to the Gospel. Jesus paid the price for the spirit of man to be made alive. It is the application of the work of Christ that makes the spirit alive by uniting it with the Holy Spirit to form the new creature. Apostle Paul talked about this connection in Romans Chapter 8. Spiritual formation is the process of the integration and proper alignment of the body, soul, and spirit. The new creature and the new creature's expression are in opposition to the lusting of the flesh. Bringing all areas of the human experience into subjection to the leading of the Holy Spirit is spiritual health.

The church, like a person, has a body, soul, and spirit. The same application of spiritual wellbeing for the individual applies to the church. The church is to love God and love people with all they have. This process of integration is the task of all believers. For the Body of Christ to grow up into all aspects of Jesus, each part should be working correctly and under the authority of Christ. This amalgamation needs to be taken into consideration as we look at spiritual health. This interplay of body, soul, and spirit necessitates correct priorities and hierarchical position if the proper spiritual formation is to occur. Misalignment or lack of Holy Spirit domination will result in corruption.

As the brain operates naturally bottom-up/right to left, the spirit, soul, and body operate best as the human spirit is guided by the Holy Spirit to direct the soul. This ability to follow the Holy Spirit then instructs the mind and body. Any misalignment of this priority structure results in deception and sin. The Holy Spirit uses the Scripture to bring thoughts to mind helping counsel the soul bringing behavior into obedience to God's precepts. The human conscience is like a clock; it may work, but if it is not set to the right spiritual time, the result will be each man doing what is right in his own eyes. The Holy Spirit uses the power of God's Word to set the conscience back to the correct *spiritual time*. Using God's Scripture then becomes one of the most important Spiritual Life Design Protocols (SLDP). All of this begins with repentance and self-reductionism.

The left side of the brain is used to encode the written Word into the brain. Through the power of Biblical meditation, this logical written encoded word is processed through to the right side (the emotional side of the brain). Meditation and solitude then become another very important SLDP. These two protocols will be discussed in detail in chapter 6. As a result of proper meditation, the heart is touched which brings conviction as it interacts with the new creature within. The Holy Spirit bears witness to the truth and brings a changed mind where needed, and then behavior or outward holiness is achieved.

The mechanisms of temptation within the follower, for instance, demonstrates this tripartite interaction between the body, soul, and spirit. Jesus teaches His disciples in Chapter 6 of the Book of Matthew, how to pray. He begins the chapter by explaining how not to pray and the results of being religious for "show." In verse 9, He tells His disciples,

"Pray, then, in this way: 'Our Father who is in heaven, hallowed be Your name. Your kingdom come. Your will be done, on earth

as it is in heaven. Give us this day our daily bread. And forgive us our debts, as we also have forgiven our debtors. And do not lead us into temptation but deliver us from evil. For Yours is the kingdom and the power and the glory forever. Amen.'"[93]

In the instructions of Jesus, He explains that His believers are to pray to God for protection against being led into temptation. Recently, the phrase "Lead us not into temptation but deliver us from evil" came under concern by Pope Francis of Assisi (Jorge Mario Bergoglio). He stated that he thought that people are getting the wrong theological idea about God because of this phrase. The Pope decided that the Scripture needed to be changed.

At first glance, this part of the Lord's prayer seems to indicate God the Father is actively involved in taking His followers toward temptation. It is important to know one of the principles of hermeneutics* concerning understanding a difficult or important portion of Scripture. This principle states, to get the correct interpretation to an unclear verse you must look at other Scriptures dealing with the same subject. According to Apostle James,

Blessed is a man who perseveres under trial; for once he has been approved, he will receive the crown of life which the Lord has promised to those who love Him. Let no one say when he is tempted, "I am being tempted by God"; for God cannot be tempted by evil, and He Himself does not tempt anyone.† *But each one is tempted when he is carried away and enticed by his lust. Then when lust has conceived, it gives birth to sin; and when sin is accomplished, it brings forth death. Do not be deceived, my beloved brethren. Every good thing given and every perfect gift is from above, coming down from the Father of lights, with whom there is no variation or shifting shadow. In*

---

* *Hermeneutics is the science or methodology of Biblical interpretation.*
† *Emphasis added by author.*

the exercise of His will He brought us forth by the word of truth, so that we would be a kind of first fruits among His creatures.[94]

This passage clearly states that God will not tempt anyone. The question remains, "what is Jesus asking us to pray?" The optimum word in this part of the Lord's Prayer is "lead." Lead is the root word for leadership. Leadership, at its simplest meaning, is an influence. The problem with temptation is an influence. The believer is to ask the Father to keep the influencers in his life edifying and not negative (not tempting). The question is then, "what are the influencers in the follower's life?" Influencers in a person's life are many. A person can be swayed by others, themselves, entertainment, media, and leaders. The remedy for temptation, which demonstrates the interactions between the body, soul and spirit systems, is again found in James. He states,

What is the source of quarrels and conflicts among you? Is not the source your pleasures that wage war in your members? You lust and do not have; so you commit murder. You are envious and cannot obtain; so you fight and quarrel. You do not have because you do not ask. You ask and do not receive, because you ask with wrong motives, so that you may spend it on your pleasures. You adulteresses, do you not know that friendship with the world is hostility toward God? Therefore, whoever wishes to be a friend of the world makes himself an enemy of God. Or do you think that the Scripture speaks to no purpose: 'He jealously desires the Spirit which He has made to dwell in us'? But He gives a greater grace. Therefore, it says, "GOD IS OPPOSED TO THE PROUD, BUT GIVES GRACE TO THE HUMBLE." Submit therefore to God. Resist the devil and he will flee from you. Draw near to God and He will draw near to you. Cleanse your hands, you sinners; and purify your hearts, you double-minded. Be miserable and mourn and weep; let your laughter be turned into mourning and your joy to gloom. Humble yourselves in the presence of the Lord, and He will exalt you.[95]

The antidote to falling into temptation is submitting to God, which is an act of humility; resisting the devil, which is an act of character; drawing near to God, which is an act of attention and affection; and cleansing the hands, which is an act of obedience. The leading factor in this set of commands is, "drawing near to God." Drawing near to God is the action of the soul that uses the force of the will to direct the mind to control its attention. The soul uses the bidirectional control to will the mind to focus on either the flesh or the spirit. This attention leads to the affection that gives the follower direction or, leading. It is this direction that leads to "position."

> The antidote to falling into temptation is submitting to God, which is an act of humility; resisting the devil, which is an act of character; drawing near to God, which is an act of attention and affection; and cleansing the hands, which is an act of obedience.

There are two basic positions or directions of the will — first, the position that places the believer "minding" the things of the flesh that leads to death. Secondly, the position that places the follower "minding the things of the spirit" that leads to life.[96] This second position stations the individual in such a way to receive the presence and power of God. The location then becomes the place of mind transformation. The locus of control* of the believer is limited to the directing or the willingness of the mind toward God.

As stated previously, the energy mechanisms that interplay between the body, soul, and spirit I term, the "Reciprocal Cybernetic Interactional

---

* *Locus of control is the notion or perception that the individual is the source of control of differing situations. The proposition here is that believers have limits to their control and must depend upon God as the ultimate external locus of control.*

Inductance Hypothesis" (RCIIH).[*] These energies are separate, proximal but parallel systems and control forces interacting between the body, soul, and spirit. The universe operates off of and is energy. God used the Dunamis[†] power to create everything. The energy systems that are used between the body, soul, and spirit affect each other. These varying systems employ different source frequencies and modalities of energy. For instance, the hypothesis of the psychon[‡] or the idea of molecules of emotions[§][97] unitizes differing energy systems but interplay according to design. The psychon is a hypothetical particle of conscience that influences the person, and the other is a molecule that is derived from feelings of emotions that act upon body, soul, and spirit. For instance, when unforgiveness is harbored it leads to bitterness. Unforgiveness not only brings rottenness to the physical body but spiritually defiles self and others.[98] The point here is to demonstrate the interplay of the integrated systems of the body, soul, and spirit using varying energies.

In the chart (figure 4.1), these systems consist of the body, soul, and spirit. All these structures have a focus that produces differing controls, forces, and results. The key to this chart is seen in the bi-directional ability of the soul to focus on the spirit or the flesh. The soul uses the force of the will to direct the mind toward the attention desired, if the soul "minds" the things of the flesh, death in many areas is the result. The result can be relational death, situational death, the death of virtue and character, physical death or spiritual death. The important factor is to understand that all the Life Design Protocols (LDP) are affected by this dynamic. Throughout the book, examples will demonstrate this reality. As a bus schedule is used to locate the time and position to catch the correct bus, the soul uses these forces to place the individual at the

---

[*] *RCIIH—separate, proximal but parallel system and control forces interacting between the body, soul, and spirit.*

[†] *Dunamis—the Greek word for the Holy Spirit in many cases. It is the word we derive the word dynamite from.*

[‡] *Psychon—hypothetical particle of conscience.*

[§] *Molecules of Emotions—referenced in the book by that title describing the link between consciousness, mind, and body.*

right "bus stop" at the right time. The power is not at the bus stop; it is on the bus. In this analogy, the bus schedule represents the Word of God. The Bible gives the follower the information needed to get into the correct position to get on the right bus. Without the Scriptures, the direction to the stop is unknown. Getting on the wrong bus is analogous to getting on the bus of the world and getting the result of death. The "God bus stop" positions the believer towards life and uses His divine design.

Influencers				
System	Focus	Control	Force	Result
Body	Flesh	Physical	Desire	Death
Soul	Self/God	Mind	Will	Position
Spirit	God	Connection	Holy Spirit	Life

Fig. 4.1 Chart of interactions between body, soul, and spirit

This interflow of this reaction allows for the spiritual maturity of the followers. The outcome of this correct position (or bus stop) enables the follower to become "doers of the Word" not merely encoders. Doing the Word may be difficult, due to the many effects of sin on the human experience, as many are overloaded with the standard Western way of living. Such things as improper Physical Life Design protocols (PLDP) may cause complicated interactions resulting in sin. The PLDP use of bodily discipline, marginal management, restorative sleep, nutri-genomics, IPNB, hydration, and environmental exposure may help or derail the spiritual growth process. The Spiritual Life Design Protocols (SLDP) of self-reductionism, Sabbath keeping, solitude, meditation, connectivity, contemplation, and munificence must be taken seriously for the proper development of a healthy spiritual life which is interlocked with every aspect of human existence and health. The separation of the spiritual and the secular is incorrect. As humans, we are holistically designed to interconnect and unify. Unity underscores the importance of integrating PLDP with SLDP, which falls under the general topic of Life Design Protocols (LDP).

In the same way, the church is both physical and spiritual. The church has a body, a soul and operates by the Spirit. The same protocol dynamics apply to ensure the vitality of the congregation of God's children. The Godhead itself is the pattern of this triune nature. The Father expresses His will (soul), the Son is the physicality of God (body), and the Holy Spirit demonstrates the spiritual nature of God (spirit). God is a Spirit, and His Spirit is love. He demonstrates this complete holistic-holy unity and oneness. We have been made in His image; however, His image has been marred by the result of man's sin. This disconnection and disintegration are the cause of poor spiritual and physical health.

Reintegration and reconciliation are the work of the Holy Spirit as He applies God's Word in an all-inclusive way to man. First, to the spirit of a man making him a new creature; forgiven, and righteous before God because of the finished work of Christ. Next, the Holy Spirit empowers the believer to bring his soul into subjection to God's will. Lastly, the Holy Spirit brings correct mental orientation through the power of bringing all thoughts under the correction of the Scripture. The result is the sanctification of the entire body, soul, and spirit. The ultimate design of God is to bring results (fruit) to maturity. It is possible for the follower to have a saved spirit but a carnal walk. Carnality is spiritual immaturity. The believer is to grow up in all ways to look and act like Christ. Bringing fruit to maturity is the goal of healthy spiritual growth.

In the same way, the call on the church is to help the equipping of the individual members into maturity — not only the salvation aspect but the working out of liberation in all areas. In Romans 12:1 it states that the transformation process included renewing of the mind. A believer's thoughts brought captive to God's thoughts will reset the human fallen mind and help to bring the person into integration.

Some churches would be satisfied if everyone did externally holy behavior. They reach solely for the goal of outward conformity. Behavioral conformity is helpful only if the source of conformity is the heart, mind, soul, and body as the total person is loving Jesus and loving others. Cultural, parental, societal, religious, and shame-driven forces are cheap substitutes for life transformation. The only true lasting change in thoughts and behavior comes from life transformation. Salvation must be taken to all levels of the integrated person to produce "fruit that remains." Any source other than Jesus and abiding in Him will result in artificial fruit.

Jesus came to redeem the souls of men. He calls out to His church to be set apart. The application of redemption of the soul is the work of the Holy Spirit. As the Holy Spirit applies the Truth of God to the innermost parts of the follower, this transformation materializes. The Spirit asks us to join Him in this endeavor. The soul is the connection between the human spirit and the physicality of the human experience. The spirit that has been made alive is oriented towards God's Spirit. The spirit of man is connected to the soul. This union is hard to differentiate without the Word of God. It takes God's surgeon-like sharp Word to divide the two.[99] The spiritual growth of both the church and the individual is sourced by minding the things of the Spirit rather than the things of the flesh. "Minding" is giving attention to an object. God's Spirit within the believer is very quiet whereas the flesh is loud and attention-grabbing. Developing the ability to hear and give attention to the Spirit takes discipline. The SLDP are designed to help train the follower's spiritual senses to mind the things of the Spirit. This dance of opposition between the flesh and the spirit is the tension facing every believer. It takes focused attention towards God's Word and His Spirit to apply the needed power for correct spiritual growth. The movement from awareness to attention to activation leads to affection and action towards either the flesh or the spirit. Spiritual growth is accomplished as the attention leads to affection for God and correct positioning to receive His empowerment and subsequent true spiritual growth.

3 BRAINS

The soul connects to the Holy Spirit and the person's total being. The soul gets its human input from the brain, heart, and gut. All three have neurons that attach them interactively to the rest of the body. The mind and soul are a mixture of the operations of the brain, heart, and gut. All three areas of the body have unique purposes and functions that input into the soul, and the soul directs and applies correction when it is surrendered to God's Spirit. The latest studies in epigenetics, biophotonics,[*] and interpersonal neural biology all point to an interplay of all three of these "brains." This total mind controls varying aspects of the human experience. We will explore more of these interplays in chapter 6. The SLDP play an indispensable part in integrating the body, soul, and spirit. The outcome of this spiritual strength loves God with all of one's being and others as themselves.

The soul is the essence of the person. It controls the gates of the will, focus, and attention. These, in turn, allow movement of affection and emotions. The soul uses the mind to formulate the direction of the will to apply effort to focus on either the fleshly or spiritual nature of the person. One direction leads to death and the other to life. The soul gains strength through the stimulation of the physical body or the spirit man made alive by God's Spirit. It is thus important for the soul to be subjugated to the Holy Spirit which has made the new creature alive by activating the spirit of man. The soul, under the

> It is thus important for the soul to be subjugated to the Holy Spirit which has made the new creature alive by activating the spirit of man.

---

[*] *The biophotonic nature of the energetic capabilities of the heart to emit lazar-like emissions to imprint DNA causing methylation and histone modification.*

power of the Holy Spirit, can then direct the rest of the person to come in line with the life of God and worship Him with total body, soul, and spirit. When the soul of a person is bound up by lies and sin, the person tends toward carnality. This person is considered "soulish." When the fleshly desires direct the soul, it suppresses the new creature and the Spirit of God. Giving into fleshly desires is the fruit of an immature follower.

At the operational level, intense discipleship (counseling) may be seen best as the ability to witness to the Holy Spirit's design of pointing to God's redemptive Word as the answer to life issues. Every area of life needs to be taken into consideration if the counselor is to help guide the disciple into all truth. It is the truth that sets people free. Not just the saying of truth, but truth applied to every part of life. Soul care is very complicated because of the need to deal with the whole person. Their spiritual, emotional, mental, physiological and life routines all must be taken into consideration. Spiritual Life Design Protocols are of little value if the PLDP are relentlessly violated. The wellbeing of the total person must be addressed. In the same way, the Church is spiritual, but it is not purely spiritual. Proper life and spiritual priorities account for the ability of the person and the Church to function as God intended.

When applying intense discipleship such as counseling, life coaching, or pneuma-energeticpsychobio interaction factor (PEPBIF) healing,[*] the total person must be considered. Their current life situation, life

---

[*] *Pneuma-energeticpsychobio interaction factor healing is the counseling descriptor used in the emotional healing of locked up incorrect emotional responses due to imbedded lies inserted during the developmental stages of childhood growth. Schemas with locked up memory blocks caused by false interpretations of one's safety, purpose, value or future expectations and future image are changed using the Holy Spirit's guidance to exchange the believed lie with the truth. These imprintings are usually developed between the ages of pre-birth and 14 years. Inserting the proper interpretations into the faulty memory block frees the person. The principle of pneuma-energeticpsychobio interaction factor (PEPBIF) is the realignment of the body, soul and spirit hierarchy whereas the spirit of the person is empowered by the Holy Spirit to lead them in all aspects of life. Proper PEPBIF allows for deep healing to take place and is the proper functioning of the follower's daily LDP. Minding the things of the spirit increases truth in the inner man. ("you will know the truth and the truth will set you free").*

image-projective outlook, as well and their developmental past must be examined. Separating and fragmenting the person into nonintegrated parts will not allow for proper instruction in discipleship and deep counseling. As Jesus dealt with His disciples and disciple wannabe's, we can observe His holistic approach. Jesus challenged not only the spiritual nature of the person but the soul, family dynamics, employment, as well as, emotional healing. As Jesus healed one of His closest disciples, Peter, we can detect how Jesus used the smell of charcoaling fish to trigger the painful memory of Peter's denial emotionally. Jesus used the physical triggering of smell to reach past Peter's prefrontal cortex (logic center) to penetrate directly into His disciples locked up memory of shame which leads to Peter's healing. Peter was then able to "feed My sheep."[100]

The health of individual souls will translate into a healthy church. Because the soul has many forces acting upon it, it is critical for the leader to understand how these forces operate and how to help disciple people toward health and maturity. It is imperative for the leader to have a healthy physical, emotional, psychological and spiritual life too. Following the LDP does not imply self-help or human effort but the ability to move successfully in the area of self-reduction. Denying one's self and picking up the cross-life will lead to "abiding in His vine." Jesus demonstrated through His life the concept of the cross-life. If Jesus applied the SLDP in His walk, how much more should we? His followers are to point to His example with their lives. It's not about adding something more to do in our lives but reducing the negative factors and embracing the life force of His Spirit. There are too many distractions and complications in our post-modern world to add more to the plate of the disciple. Simplifying by radically eliminating the complications of our day through marginal management will allow us to hear the voice of the Holy Spirit the same way Jesus did. If we expect to do what Jesus did, we must live the SLDP the way He did.

In a Western culture with the orientation of self-reliance, self-aggrandizement, self-absorption, a self-recalcitrant attitude, and self-protection it is little wonder, so many followers find it hard to hear the message of self-reductionism. The soul; however, that is attuned to the things of the Spirit will develop neurogenesis[*] resulting in a new way of thinking. There is the great hope for the follower with this new spirit power to change the directional progress of their spiritual growth. It is not as if there is a constant tug of war with equally strong opposing forces. When God feeds the soul, transformation takes place. It is easier than most people realize. It seems that the war of opposing sides has equal power and at times as if the "good side" is somewhat weaker. The reality is that as the spirit grows it has an unstoppable power that can even suppress and overcome the strongest of fleshly temptations. As the spirit man grows through reduc-

> As the spirit man grows through reductionism of the old man, even the physical body changes the cybernetic responses, and new feedback loops are employed. These forces within the physical body, when subjugated to the power of the Holy Spirit help regulate physiological states.

tionism of the old man, even the physical body changes the cybernetic responses, and new feedback loops are employed. These forces within the physical body, when subjugated to the power of the Holy Spirit help regulate physiological states.

The soul, resting and empowered by God, transmits a positive dialogue throughout the entire person that creates peace that passes understanding. Soul-rest is a biological imperative of the new connections. The soul, under the unbridled lawless flesh (physical impulses), acts like the Tasmanian Devil[†]—an unabated search of new flesh to consume. Finding Jesus is finding peace and eternal satisfaction. When the flesh is under subjection to the spirit, God consecrates it and allows

---

[*] *Neurogenesis is the birthing of new neurons through neuroplasticity of the brain. This allows for a new way of thinking transformatively which can even produce new genetic expressions physiologically.*
[†] *It has been recorded that the Tasmanian Devil will cover 10 miles a night looking for food.*

it to be used for its intended purpose—the glorifying of His goals. The human soul has tremendous potential when submitted to the Holy Spirit. Conversely, the soul can also house a hoard of demonic spirits if given over to the lust and narcissistic drives of self. Repentance is the first step towards this redemptive process of God's empowerment. Realizing the hopelessness of self-effort is a good first step. The dashing of hope placed on the flesh will lead you to the One True Hope. He is closer than you think and vastly more powerful than you can imagine. He can transform your entire life, body, soul, and spirit. Surrender your hope in everything except His unfailing love. The spiritual health of your soul and your church depends upon this. The world needs to see spiritual maturity.

"The spirit of a man is the lamp of the Lord, searching
all the innermost parts of his being."
Proverbs 20:27

4.2 BACKDROP

RockFish Church is located in the military area of Fort Bragg. Fort Bragg brings with it people from all over the world. The population is made up of mostly young families. These families experience tremendous pressures and struggles. The families of RockFish face not only the challenges of raising young children but an array of practical obstacles. The problems of multiple deployments, changing duty stations and navigating new locations, along with the stress of the current war, all have led to the necessity of developing a church that meets needs involving a kaleidoscope of life's complications. Over the last 25 years, the yearly turnover rate of RockFish has been 25% or more. Due to changes in duty stations, the exiting from active duty, and retirements, the church has had to adapt to influx and depletion. People also come from varying religious expressions and experiences. These variables along with the southern religious structures of this part of North Carolina make for a unique expression of the body of Christ. Spiritual health in this changing dynamic allows for leadership growth and stretching.

The challenges of an ever-changing congregation that has stayed relatively young created an exciting and difficult experience. The importance of staying "close to the cross" with life application-type messages became the foundational emphasis of the weekend messages. As the church grew, philosophical ideas were formed around the Biblical principle of building squarely upon the foundation of Jesus and His teachings. Priorities, values, and expectations were cross-checked and rechecked against this foundation. The philosophy of ministry was kept simple. The Gospel, Christ's teachings, and doing life with people of diverse backgrounds and histories was the lens through which the leadership was charged to oversee. The structure of leadership will be discussed in greater detail in chapter 7.

Service delivery (practical ministry application) was accomplished keeping the values and the philosophy of Gospel-centered mission in focus. The three main driving forces steering RockFish Church are the value of a family-friendly, multiculturally-diverse, military-embracing ministry. It was important to have a strategy that clarified the mission of RockFish Church with quick assimilation and ease of departure. This concept led to creating an open, inviting drive-by first impression. The main evangelism tool utilized is the outside appearance. As people look at the church while passing by, the goal of the look was to communicate our identity as clearly as possible. When asked the question to newcomers in our "Starting Point" class, "Why did you pick RockFish Church?" the number one reported reason was "yellow umbrellas." The third-space area across the front of the building is designed to give it a welcoming, come as you are feeling. This space has a long canopy arranged with outdoor seating for about a hundred people. Each table sports a bright yellow umbrella, a napkin holder with ministry information, and video displays overhead. There are many other reasons given for a first-time guest's attendance, but this one tops them all. I am not suggesting churches run out and buy yellow decorations, but simply to understand the mission God has uniquely given to each church and find a way to speak that to the outdoor community even without using words.

Inside RockFish Church the guests find easy access to information and entry locations pointing to everything from the children's ministry to the restrooms. Four welcome centers are operated throughout the six weekly services. Service broadcasting monitors are located inside and out for the "in service" experience as people arrive on the property. The services always start five minutes early with a countdown. The purpose of starting five minutes before the actual published time is derived from the military mindset that if you are not five minutes early, you are late, and it allows for a call to worship from the front of the stage followed by a personal welcome in between the first and second song. One of the noticeable events of the worship experience is baptism. Baptisms are offered during all services. The worship style is contemporary/vertical. The Director of Worship parallels worship songs directed toward magnifying Jesus that are played on the local Christian radio station. Performing the same songs as the radio station allows the music to reach people through the week and helps the worshippers know the words to the songs. Knowing the words to the songs helps create a more natural worship experience. Free freshly-ground coffee, as well as iced tea, are offered throughout the venue. Drinks, entire families, and attire variations are all allowed in the worship center. In Chapter 6 we will look deeply into how worship is metabolized.

RockFish employs small groups called "RockGroups" to allow for personal discipleship and ministry. One of the best ways the church has stayed feeling small while growing larger is discovered in RockGroups. Doing life together to make the Name of Jesus greater known is the main idea behind these groups. The themes of RockGroups may differ, but the main objective is the same, loving Jesus and others. These groups need constant attention at RockFish due to the constant movement of the military community. They are very important for the same reason. Spiritual growth never totally happens solo. People need people, and research demonstrates that in the same way there is no such thing as an individual neuron, there is no such thing as an individual brain. The brain of one needs the brain of another by design. Lives only work by design as they relate to others in a meaningful way. The field of study that explores this concept is called Interpersonal Neurobiology*(IPNB). An example of how IPNB works can be seen in an example explained by Dr. Thompson in his book entitled *The Soul of Shame* when he states,

> What is the interpersonal neurobiological nature of shame? It is critical to note from the outset that shame as a neurophysiologic phenomenon is not bad in and of itself. It is, rather, our system's way of warning of possible impending abandonment, although we do not think of it in those terms, and certainly not at early ages. However, our problem with it is generally that we tend to respond to it relationally moving away from others rather than towards them, while experiencing within our own minds a similar phenomenon of internal disintegration. Moreover, our response is largely a function of how we collaborate—or don't—with the relational capital we share with others that, when accessed appropriately, will lead to growth and connection.[101]

IPNB carries with it the idea, as we interact with others, that parallel forces are influencing the body, soul, and spirit. The interplay between people is a necessary LDP factor that should be considered when desiring healthy spiritual growth. IPNB is one of the important PLDP that will be discussed in greater detail in chapter 8. A study in IPNB would be a good course for a small group director or pastor to take. The principles of this theory, although not purely Christian, help explain God's design as it relates to relationships. Becoming familiar with the concept of the importance of good fellowship would assist not only the spiritual but psychological well-being of the

> IPNB carries with it the idea, as we interact with others, that parallel forces are influencing the body, soul, and spirit.

---

* *Interpersonal Neural Biology (IPNB) is the concept that people need others not only emotionally but in all facets of human experience. This interdisciplinary field of study was developed by Dan J. Siegel, M.D. and Allen Schore.*

congregation.

RockFish has become larger than she was a few years ago, so one of the main efforts has been to focus on making the atmosphere of the church feel smaller. This effort to maintain closeness has led to some innovative structures. Besides RockGroups, the church has two services a week designed to propagate fellowship and a family feel. During the Friday and Saturday night services, Café Rock feeds attendees free of charge. The entire worship center is transformed each week into circular table seating. The menu includes cheeseburgers or chicken sandwiches, French fries, drinks, and two choices of green mixed salads. One salad is topped with grilled chicken strips, and one salad is vegan (with or without cheese and croutons). (A change was recently made to Café Rock due to this study. I had all the drinks containing high fructose corn syrup removed. Instead, we purchased a water purifier that gives the people the best water possible). The service is structured with worship, baptism, and teaching. Eating together as a smaller group allows for the smaller fellowship-type experience. The sermon is the same as the Sunday services. During Café Rock, no offering is taken. This ministry has seen people from all walks of life ranging from the homeless to members of other churches looking for extra fellowship and "breaking of the bread together" experience. To date, Café Rock has fed 100,000 people since it began six years ago.

In August 2017, RockFish Church began offering baptism twenty-four hours a day, seven days a week. Billboards were busy with the message of baptisms 24/7 on main highways leading into North Carolina. The result was astounding. Truck drivers, workers, and disenfranchised followers came to repent and make a public profession of faith in Jesus. Two hundred forty-seven people were baptized in approximately two months through this effort. The structure that allowed for this offer was simple. An on-call senior staff member operated the phones to receive the calls, and they, in turn, informed their team. The teams were made up of at least one senior staff, one governmental leader, and one support staff. An alert would go out through the church app, before the call for baptism. Having a call to baptism invites any member to participate and witness the event. Even during a sermon, if someone repented and wanted baptism, the service would focus on celebrating with the hosts of heaven. The 24/7 baptism continues as part of the culture of RockFish Church.

Emphasis is placed on all five general purposes. Worship, fellowship, evangelism, discipleship, and ministry are closely watched and kept in balance. The outworking of this philosophy may take many different forms when applied to other churches. Taking practices alone will NOT ensure a healthy, growing church. The theological truths must never change. The philosophical application of theology will tell the why of the practice. Practice touches the culture. The Lord is about redeeming people and the culture. The philosophy ties the theology to the practice. These must properly relate to good Biblical theology and teaching. If the teachings of Scripture are violated to affirm cultural values, gross error and church sickness are inevitable. The test for leadership today is to discern which cultural values to affirm and which to expose as needing redemption. It is also important for church leadership to model a Biblical lifestyle and examine their walk with all soberness.

RockFish Church has faced many challenges over the years, but the greatest force for distraction is the cultural shift of the past ten years or so. The sexual rebellion is just the symptom of people pulling away from God and His instruction to follow after their desires. Teachers are being raised up in the modern culture that takes advantage of the wishes of people. The church must grow spiritually mature and offer truth without compromise while doing so in a culturally relevant way. Jesus is the perfect model of reaching, teaching, healing, and living needed to accomplish the delivery of the Gospel message to every culture for redemption. It is the followers' time to shine brightly in a darkened world. Spiritually healthy and mature groups of followers can win the day and see the mighty hand of God work miracles. It takes radically abandoned people, given to His work, to see the Gospel advanced.

4.3 HISTORY

RockFish, as it is seen today, was relaunched in 2007. The original church was called Raeford Christian Fellowship (and remains the corporate name today). Raeford Christian Fellowship (RCF) was founded by Joe Rodrigues (Pastor), Kevin Gheen (Elder in training), me (Elder in training), and a total of eleven families. The Church was planted by Pastor Michael Fletcher of Manna Church of Fayetteville, North Carolina in 1991. Pastor Joe became ill in 1993 and was unable to continue. At the time, I was working in vocational rehabilitation. The church asked me to assume the role of Senior Permanent Pastor after being the Interim Pastor in a bi-vocational capacity. On August 28, 1994, I was set in as the Senior Pastor.

I served in the military for six years (four years of active duty) and was in the process of using my GI bill to complete my education. In December 1996, I became the full-time Pastor. I finished my Ph.D. in Christian Counseling Psychology May 2, 1998. I began counseling for different local churches and worked toward bringing Raeford Christian Fellowship toward her God-given call. Through the teachings of the Purpose Driven Church written by Rick Warren, I worked on trying to figure out how to lead this small, but a fully devoted group of people. I changed the name to RockFish Church because it became evident that we needed to communicate a clear message of the identity of the church. I wanted a name that was easy enough for a five-year-old to remember. By this time, we had moved from rented houses to schools, and to stand-alone commercial buildings. Most of our congregation came from a community called "Rockfish."

Through a series of events, my wife and I felt like we needed to sell everything we had to buy a piece of land to relocate the church in the center of the traffic area of Rockfish and Fort Bragg's back entrance. The property had a house for us to live in with seven acres on the main highway. Before constructing the building, the leadership decided to go with a company that asked us to sell a piece of the land to them and let them build to suit a new building that we could buy back from them after we got it up and going. The current building RockFish meets in is that building. Since then we have added classrooms and a total of thirty-five acres at the same location. We plan on building a larger worship center soon. Our current facility seats five hundred inside and another one hundred people outside, when the weather permits. The new worship center is planned to seat two thousand along with nursery and a large parking lot. From the original eleven families, the church has grown to over twenty-nine hundred. We currently hold six worship services to accommodate the people. Approximately thirty to forty new families visit RockFish Church each week.

4.4 SUSTAINABILITY

"Therefore I run in such a way, as not without aim; I box in such a way, as not beating the air; but I buffet my body and make it my slave, lest possibly, after I have preached to others, I myself should be disqualified."
1 Corinthians 9:26-27

Church life, as in life itself, is not a straight line. The oscillation and seasons of life produce a rhythm that must be understood. Traversing these seasons with success demands wisdom that comes from Above. One of the greatest gifts to the church is the leadership gift of wisdom. Knowing what Biblical principle to apply to any given situation becomes mandatory when leading yourself or others into spiritual growth that will last. Much has already been said about the importance of healthy growth, but one of the biggest indicators is the sustainability of that growth throughout the seasons of life. The goal of Jesus is for His people to finish well and fulfill their exclusive but collective call.

The first step in maintaining growth is the ability to recognize and accept the movement of times. Farmers know this very well. Doing the right thing at the wrong time will not result in a good harvest. The book of Proverbs speaks of the sluggard. Proverbs talks about the sluggard 12 times. At first reading, a person may come away with the idea that it is just talking about a lazy person. But on closer examination the larger idea becomes clear. *Go to the ant, you sluggard; consider its ways and be wise! It has no commander, no overseer or ruler, yet it stores its provisions in summer and gathers its food at harvest. How long will you lie there, you sluggard? When will you get up from your sleep?*[102] And, *The sluggard does not plow after the autumn, so he begs during the harvest and has nothing. A plan in the heart of a man is like deep water, but a man of understanding draws it out.*[103]

The problem here is not only being self-absorbed and lazy but doing the right thing at the wrong time. Lack of an understanding when to plow, seed, repair, and harvest in church life may cause low or no product of spiritual life. Pray for wisdom, and not just understanding, as you lead the church. Be like the men of Issachar. *And of the sons of Issachar, men who understood the times, with knowledge of what Israel should do, their chiefs were two hundred; and all their kinsmen were at their command.*[104] Remember, we plant, water, and plow, but God causes the increase. Pray and then obey.

Ministries go through seasons, testings, and challenges. Strong spiritual growth does not always produce a certain constant numerical physical growth; however, physical growth should be increasing, or there is something wrong. Numbers count because people count to God. God is always going after people. How much each church should grow physically is only known by God. A healthy church will grow sustainably. Likewise, a follower should grow continually in his/her walk with Jesus. Spiritual growth is demonstrated by an ever-increasing love for Him and His Word. There are many reasons for not growing in love for Him and His Church. But, in this book, I prefer to focus on health and healing rather than sickness. Diagnosing a church sickness is not that difficult, but prescribing the accurate medicine is rarely achieved. Prevention of chronic spiritual sickness is the best focus.

> Numbers count because people count to God.

The Body of Christ functions similarly to the human body. Health is realized by preserving proper life protocols. In the area of PLDP, research has demonstrated that physical health is 70% preserved by life choices. Sickness of the hereditary type accounts for less than 30%. Most factors are in our control. Learning to control the things we can control and giving the uncontrollable over to God will help reduce undue stress. The Holy Spirit was given to help us learn to function with the fruit of self-control. Self-control and self-regulation are as much about knowing and doing the correct number of good things as knowing what not to do. Working in the field of God's inheritance is an exciting thing. The key then is knowing when and how much of the good thing needs to be done now. Going to the entire world with the Gospel is the biggest task imaginable. It takes purpose, planning, and pacing to achieve this call. Understanding the thresholds of ministry and resources is important in making it to the end and completing the good works God has foreordained for each to walk in. To have sustained health, whether in a church or a human body, is a matter of following God's design.

> To have sustained health, whether in a church or a human body, is a matter of following God's design.

Violation of the God-given LDP will result in sickness and burnout. Much of the values of the post-modern culture deplete spiritual, emotional, and mental reserves. People in our culture tend to max out every area of life. This lack of backup resources becomes evident as soon as trauma or major event takes place in the life of the follower. Without proper reduction of energy outlay, most believers collapse when added stress is encountered. Holistic resiliency capacity is a matter of building marginal backup energy into all parts of the body, as well as the soul, and spirit. Remember, this is not a self-help book that adds one more thing to your already full life; it's about flowing with God's design and relying on His power to live through you. Cooperating with His plan will reduce your activity and increase your resiliency for His purposes. Stop and pray right now for God to show you what areas you need to turn from and turn over to Him.

4.5 SPIRIT LIFE

"But if the Spirit of Him who raised Jesus from the dead dwells in you, He who raised Christ Jesus from the dead will also give life to your mortal bodies through His Spirit who dwells in you. So then, brethren, we are under obligation, not to the flesh, to live according to the flesh—for if you are living according to the flesh, you must die; but if by the Spirit you are putting to death the deeds of the body, you will live. For all who are being led by the Spirit of God, these are sons of God."
Romans 8:11-14

Much of the difficulty in counseling is sourced in people following the impulses of self. Our western society propagates hedonics,* eudaimonics,† self-indulgence, self-aggrandizement, individualism, consumerism, over-the-top entertainment, amusement, etc. making up the "me culture." Dying to self and minding the Spirit is rarely found, let alone taught. The improper message of "come as you are and stay just like you are," is becoming the church norm. God loves us right where we are and loves us enough not to leave us there. God desires transformation. Following the Spirit is God's design. When a person submits to be a follower of Jesus, God sends His Holy Spirit to birth the person's spirit which forms the new creature. The Holy Spirit then begins the work of sanctification, or in other words, He works towards the integration of the whole person. He aims to sanctify us entirely. The last task of the redemptive process is the redeeming of the whole person into realizing full adoption. Full adoption will take place as the person looks Jesus directly in the face when in heaven. As the Holy Spirit works on every area of our lives, it is our part to mind the things of the Spirit. According to Romans 8:5-8,

---

* Hedonics is the philosophy of life that celebrates pleasure over discomfort and pain.
† Eudaimonics, pronounced "you-demonics" is concerned with self-actualization and wellbeing.

For those who are according to the flesh set their minds on the things of the flesh, but those who are according to the Spirit, the things of the Spirit. For the mind set on the flesh is death, but the mind set on the Spirit is life and peace, because the mind set on the flesh is hostile toward God; for it does not subject itself to the law of God, for it is not even able to do so, and those who are in the flesh cannot please God.

Teaching a person to work through their salvation without the Holy Spirit is asking the impossible. The Christian life is supernatural. The church that does not operate with the realization that, apart from Jesus it can do nothing, will result in devastation or relying on a form of religion without true life. It is critical for individuals, as well as churches, to follow the SLDP. It is imperative for a healthy spiritual life to be sourced and connected completely in and to the Power of God through His indwelling Holy Spirit. The question then is, "How can the follower cooperate with the grace of God given to him/her to become more like Christ?". Jesus spoke of taking on His yoke and learning from Him. He said it would not be a heavy load. What does this heavenly load look like from our end? What can this even mean? How do we understand this statement?

Working in and with the supernatural forces of heaven is an exciting possibility. The difficulty of simply walking with Christ is found in the very nature of God's design. Our world operates upside-down as compared to the logic of heaven. The Scripture speaks of man's way of thinking as demonic.[105] God's way of thinking is described in James 3:13-18 which says God's wisdom is pure, peaceable, gentle, reasonable, merciful, has good results, strengthening and never vacillating. God's wisdom is very different from the world's perspectives, expectations, and value structures.

In our dance with the reality of God, contrasted with our earthly ideas that are filled with the carnal expectations of life, one may overlook the obvious—that we are *all* terminal. The intention of following God's design is not living forever, or even longer for longevity itself, but being available to Him and finishing well. Unless you miss the intention of this book and mistakenly think it is a book of self-help or a way to formulate a better life here on earth, I want to be clear; our limited human lives can do nothing apart from the power of God's grace working through love. The spirit-life is a life of the ever-increasing acknowledgment of its dependency upon Jesus. When, or if, we find our lives full and satisfying in this finite existence, we may lose the real substance of it. If we lose the wonder of day to day life and this here-and-now moment, we will one day find our way down a road that leads to nothing more than regret. Walking by the Spirit is living in the amazement of the gift we have been given called life. This life can be used up like a bad 401K plan or put into the hands of the Father who created us for His pleasure.

> The intention of following God's design is not living forever, or even longer for longevity itself, but being available to Him and finishing well.

This book is written to help us make the most of the gift of life. We live, move, and have our being in Him. We dance an uncertain dance that must take the "next step" directions from the One who leads and upholds us all. Following all the LDP to the letter does *not* ensure a plan for longevity or superhuman achievement. It does, however, give us the ability to cooperate with God's design and offer our lives back to Him. We are to hold to the confession that we are not our own, but we belong to Him. Wanting to be the best one can be in Jesus is the highest pursuit of thanksgiving we can offer. By drawing near to Him and allowing this simple temple of the Holy Spirit to be used for His glory, is the duty of the follower. Living the quality of life that will allow for the availability of body, soul, and spirit brings glory to Him and His kingdom.

REAL LIFE

Waking up tomorrow to the news of the worst tragedy imaginable is a real possibility. It could be the news from a doctor about a medical condition, a car wreck, moral failure of a close friend, divorce, abuse of a child or grandchild, death of a loved one, natural disaster, or the termination of employment. We all are either headed for some form of trauma, in one right now, or coming out of one. This reality is the product of this broken world of our existence. We must live on for the glory of God. Following Jesus is not like a grand pleasure cruise. It is more like a massive rescue mission on a sinking ship that is slowly going down with only a few people acknowledging it. The philosophy of modern thinking is so engrossed in progress and man being the answer for himself that it rarely underscores the need to be rescued or the need of the Savior.

Living by the Spirit is more than spooky living. Living by the Spirit is a life lived in unhurried gratitude pointed toward the desperate need for Jesus Himself. It is a life filled with truth, mercy, and grace for those around us and becomes a guiding light. Drawing near to God is not unlike any other relationship. It takes desire, time, thinking, consideration, and thankfulness. The thought that the Grand Master of the cosmos is the Loving Father and Creator that wants to relate to us with fervent passion and unfailing love becomes a powerful driving force for daily living. Sowing to the Spirit is not "pie in the sky" hoping, it is the living of each moment while recognizing that life is a gift given. If we groan for God, we have a promise of finding Him. As you find Him, don't be shocked to find that He does not think as you do. His ways are so much higher than imaginable. His ways do not make human logical sense. This world is filled with so much unimaginable pain, suffering, death, and sickness that our logic fails to comprehend it. We want to know how He could be love and not fix this hideous condition. It is ok not to understand. Jesus promised that in this life you would have heartache and suffering. But our overcoming ability is found in trusting that He has overcome this world. Bringing this reality to bear through our lives as we live in each moment as a gift, testifies to the mystery of a loving grace-filled God. People don't get what they deserve, and from our perspective, life is not predictable, fair, consistent, or equitable.

Life by the Spirit is surrender to Him without reservation. We could do all of His designs, and we could still get an incurable disease, hit by a car, slandered, walked out on, or fail in the eyes of the world. It is in these moments that our words may speak of the unfairness of this world while proclaiming the mysteries of the loving God. Life is very hard sometimes. We are all going to die. Disappointment is around the corner. Dashed hopes may lie on the floor, yet it is possible to rejoice in the Lord. Life is not about entitlements. Life is a gift, and it does not end with our last breath. Live now. Love now. Hope in the Everlasting One. He is closer than you think.

DESIGNED FOR BETTER

The SLDP are designed to, first of all, reduce the fleshly influences on the follower and increase room for spiritual growth. The SLDP are not a to-do list. They are a refocusing of life designs. They carve out space to hear, feel, appreciate, and have a reserve to give service to others. Doing the LDP will not convince anyone there is a God or that knowing these designs will make a person into a spiritual giant. They are explained in this book to help increase the wonder of the majesty of the Father and help make us usable for His purposes.

Some may protest that they don't need to know why something works the way it does, they just read the Bible, believe God said it, and it is settled. They simply obey. I believe faith as a child is the purest form of trust. I love child-like obedience. For the person working in and with the weaknesses of humanity; however, it is encouraging to understand some of the possibilities blocking people from this simple obedience. It has been my experience that if I demonstrate to a person that I understand their feelings, weaknesses, or brokenness, they are more open and trusting to me as well as Jesus. The LDP are used to help disciplers and leaders to be the best they can be in Jesus to win some to

Him. God has a design and when the design is violated it causes unnecessary distractions and hurts. Becoming the best in Jesus is walking with Him unencumbered by the sideways energy that we find ourselves so easily putting effort into--laying aside these obstacles, that certainly set us back, is the purpose of the LDP. Making room for God in our lives is about reducing, not a to-do list. Re-prioritizing the things that we can control reduces stress which allows greater room for the Holy Spirit to move.

> Making room for God in our lives is about reducing, not a to-do list.

The SLDP of 1) self-reductionism, 2) Sabbath-observing, 3) solitude, 4) meditation, 5) connectivity, 6) contemplation and 7) munificence are all the designs created by God. These designs of God help the believer stay focused upon the true activities that are within their control. Much of what is attempted by Christians is really out of their control. Many times, believers focus on things out of their control and formulas (many times being taught by well-meaning leaders) that they believe will trigger blessings and favor from God. They may attempt to "hold their hands correctly" while praying, raise them perfectly, read the Bible the ample amount of time, and attend the gatherings with faithfulness; believing that these acts, in and of themselves, are the correct mixture for a blessing. They think that these instructions and actions can pull down His approval, and therefore, the blessed life. But, when life hands out a blow of trauma/drama, they assume (as do some onlookers) that God is displeased with them and is now punishing them for "doing it" wrong. Retribution, in this context, is not only incorrect theologically, but I recommend trading in this god for the true ONE. We all have some of this underlying notion that pain is evil and comfort is blessed. Following this thinking is called "hedonics."[*]

Others believe that all that is needed is to learn the correct way to self-actualize and this self-power makes the path ahead, the road to

_____

[*] *Hedonics is the philosophy that focuses on pain reduction and pleasure increase. Pain is evil, and pleasure is godly.*

success. Humanism teaches that the next evolution of man will involve the survival of the self-actualized. People rush to buy the next successfully trending recommendation by the buffed-out bodybuilder that claims to hold the greatest secret to the perfect body, produced by the latest organic pill, exercise routine, or yoga position, that allows you to eat everything while spending most of the time on the couch, are evidence of this belief. This philosophy is called "eudaimonics."* This worldview focuses on self and self-improvement. Becoming and making a difference for personal longevity and fulfillment are the main objectives. Words like "kindness," "empathy," making a "difference," and "compassion" are salted and peppered throughout as special philosophical mantras. In recent years, this philosophical option seems to be overtaking the hedonic approach. The reason the eudaimonic philosophical viewpoint is so popular is that at the core of human longing is the desire to be able to control it all. This prevalent cultural idea contains the notion that man is the answer and solution for himself.

Biblically speaking, the design of God for the philosophy of human life is predicated upon what I call the "cross-life." At the core of this idea is the belief that Jesus is the answer for all the issues of humanity (even if the answer is silence at times). Jesus doesn't just answer; He *is* the answer. He does not answer to us; we answer to Him. We experience life through giving and "dying" of our ways in favor of God's instructions. He designed human life and He knows how it operates. When we offer our lives as "living sacrifices" we give Him the honor He deserves. He gave us this gift of life and made it function according to His design. Knowing life this way creates the link to His heavenly world. Our attention pointed towards Him glorifies His name. Our attention leads to adoration, and this leads to the value of heaven and a priority shift regarding the eternal.

Being led by the Spirit is dying to self and minding the spirit life. Following the Spirit's leading means, a reduction of self-attention, self-

---

* Eudaimonics (pronounced "you-demonics") is the philosophy that focuses on self-well-being by discovering the importance of your personal core values.

importance, and self-activities. As a Senior Pastor, it was hard for me to reduce my pulpit time. I had to realize that the best thing for the church was not me, but Jesus and His expression through others. Jesus told His disciples, before His departure, that it was for the good of them and the world if He left. He said greater things were capable if He was taken from Earth! I can't envision if Jesus was the pastor of a church, I was a part of, and He said He had to move on, how that was, in any way, a good idea, let alone a better plan!

> The spirit-life is dying to the self-life. It is a reducing life. Self-reductionism is the first step in initializing the SLDP.

The Body of Christ is just that, a body. Many parts all growing and learning how to complete their independent parts to make the Church whole. There are no such things as individual Christians. We are complete in Him. By reducing self-importance, we mature, and the Body of Christ grows. The spirit-life is dying to the self-life. It is a reducing life. Self-reductionism is the first step in initializing the SLDP.

According to my pastor Michael Fletcher,

I believe in vision and planning and structure and all the other stuff that has to be there to make church a church. But if it's my church, then all that stuff starts with me, and I have to get the Lord to help me with it. However, if it's His church, then all that stuff starts with Him, and He enlists me to cooperate with Him. It's His vision, not my vision. It's His people, not my people.[106]

The reduction of self-importance, and giving the supremacy to Jesus building the church, transport the idea that it is not about us, not about here, and not about now. Self-reductionism keeps the leader from hindering the Holy Spirit's flow of His construction power.

The next protocol is the confusing "Sabbath Rest." Much debate references around this term and its meaning. Understanding the terms helps greatly to discover the purpose and meaning of intent. The first

Biblical reference of the term, Sabbath, is found in Exodus Chapter 16. The wording in this text seems to indicate that, even though the word was not recorded in the Scripture up to this point, the concept was historically understood. In Genesis, it states that,

> *By the seventh day God completed His work which He had done, and He rested on the seventh day from all His work which He had done. Then God blessed the seventh day and sanctified it, because in it He rested from all His work which God had created and made.*[107]

God demonstrated His design pattern of doing work in six days and resting on one. In the Hebrew, the word "rest" paints a picture of desisting or ending a project. The New Testament book of Hebrews describes the believer's relationship to the Sabbath. In Chapter 4 of Hebrews, it expands the concept of the Sabbath to include resting from all works of righteousness and relying upon the finished work of the cross. The Sabbath rest for the follower is found in Christ. The spiritual protocol of the Sabbath is not only taking one day a week to focus completely upon reconnection to God by giving Him full attention but also finding the rest of God daily in the cross-life design.

The Sabbath design is found linked with the design of one-tenth giving that is seen in all of nature. God tuned the universe to the one-tenth principle. We will cover this later with the discussion of the SLDP termed "munificence."* On the surface, there seems to be a disparity between the one week, six-day structure of the Sabbath and the one-tenth command of giving. Upon deeper study, it becomes clear that they both are parallel designs of God.

The format of the Ten Commandments gives an indicator of how we are designed to function in relationship to God, others, and ourselves. The first three commands were commands that prioritize the preeminence of God and our worship of Him alone. The last six commands

---

* *Munificence is the internal attitude which leads to the action of lavished generosity.*

were instructions on how to relate to others by loving them as ourselves. Commandment number four gives the direction, to remember and keep the Sabbath holy. Jesus instructed the teachers of the law about the purpose of the Sabbath. In Mark, Chapter 2, Jesus says, "The Sabbath was made for man, and not man for the Sabbath. So the Son of Man is Lord even of the Sabbath." The interesting thought here is that one of the ten commands was given to mankind. Even in the commands of God's design, He gives one-tenth to us! Giving is the design of the universe. The tithe is the heart of a giving God.

The question then arises about the seven-day week! Why didn't the creation of the universe take nine days? Why didn't God work nine days and rest on the tenth? If the design protocol of God is based upon the tenth system of the tithe, why isn't this reflected in the structure of creation from the beginning? The answer is found in the third PLDP of "Restorative Sleep." God never sleeps nor slumbers,[107] but man is designed to sleep. If you calculate the number of hours in a week (168 hours) and subtract the correct design for recommended restorative sleep (based upon the functioning of required brain glymphatic system*=7.2 hours), the remaining waking time is given to the Sabbath is 16.8 hours for that day. The time left after subtracting sleep is exactly one-tenth of a seven-day week given to the purpose of spiritual connection with God. God cares so much for us; He gave us the exact formula-design for spiritual health. God demonstrated this in the creation of the universe. This SLDP is as much a part of the physical universe as gravity. We are to keep the Sabbath holy.

> God cares so much for us; He gave us the exact formula-design for spiritual health.

The practical activities of the Sabbath are to desist from the normal routine, physically, emotionally, psychologically, and spiritually and focus upon reconnection to God. This forced attention toward God is vital to our spiritual health. This day was made for the spirit-man to

---

* *Glymphatic system is the functional waste removal pathway of the brain. (more on this protocol result of the PLDP; Restorative Sleep in chapter five.)*

reenergize spiritually by reconnecting with the Creator. This weekly recharging is necessary for healthy spiritual growth. It is also necessary as a part of a healthy church. Pastors and leaders need to be cognizant of over-programming activities. Communicating the need for spiritual rest is important. Having permission to rest from activities (even church activities) needs to be a part of the DNA of the congregation and modeled by the leadership.

A Sabbath rest is a day to reflect, worship, connect, contemplate, meditate, read, study, and abstain from creative activities for the 16.8 hours God provided and commanded. Everyone, including pastors, needs a day away from the normal weekly work efforts. Setting a different time aside may mean that it is important for those in the employment of ministry to disengage from the normal work undertakings such as sermon preparation. It is hard for those who give messages frequently to keep from seeing everything as a sermon illustration (This is hard to turn off). I am not suggesting that God speaks to the pastor two different messages; one for him personally and one for others. I find it impossible to separate the two because I tend to speak to others only what I have walked out personally. I think it is helpful to use personal life transformation success to teach others to connect with God. However, when the daily work activity is Bible study and sermon prep etc., turning off the notion that everything needs to be turned into a message for others becomes very difficult. The busiest day of the week for the pastor could be the Sabbath for most other followers. Finding the best day for the Sabbath rest can be challenging. The fact is all of the LDP interact and have an influence upon one another. The Sabbath Rest protocol can only be realized if there is the PLDP of Marginal Management, Restorative Sleep, and Bodily Discipline.

Akin to the Sabbath Rest SLDP is the next discipline of Solitude. Jesus models this with a passion. Many times, in the Word of God, we witness Jesus getting away to a lonely place to spend time by Himself. Solitude, the unplugging from earthly relationships and conversations, is a life-giving activity. Solitude innately can self-reduce co-dependent relationship entanglements; which are unhealthy. Solitude reinforces the follower's need for a relationship with God that supplies all the emotional needs of the heart. The IPNB effects of being alone with God, without all the distractions of other people, allows for the heart, mind, and soul to receive from God without interferences. Connection with God is life-giving and life-transforming.

This protocol is easier for some. It depends upon several factors. The factors that come into play can be personality type, perception, shame level, values, or expectational faith level. Solitude is a spiritual discipline, and its benefit comes from the strengthening of dependence upon God and the reduction of interaction with other people. Moments of reflection, meditation, and contemplation along with solitude, will result in a spiritual growth dimension that is a part of a healthy spiritual life. In our busy post-modern way of life, the consistent discipline of solitude takes planning and constant effort. Reducing the need for, and continuous interaction with other people remains a challenge. The fruit of solitude brings with it the reward of increased spiritual power, internal peace, and imparted wisdom that comes from being alone with God. Whether the follower is alone with God for a few hours or extended periods of time, even days on end, the increased God-awareness will profit the trusting believer.

It is extremely important to see all of the LDP as making one available and useful to God. Physiological, psychological, emotional, mental, spiritual, and other constraints tend to take the follower "out of the game." Availability is a key ingredient in becoming a conduit for God's power. The believer's domain of influence can be transformative when there is a clear channel for the Holy Spirit's movement. Response Repentance is more than solely turning from traditional concepts of sin. This concept includes the need for a healthy, body, soul, and spirit. The idea is that God moves through followers that have turned from making life about themselves and are moving more fully toward loving God with everything. To be healthy in every part of real-time life allows spiritual growth and the

> Availability is a key ingredient in becoming a conduit for God's power.

advancement of God's kingdom. Individuals and churches that have harnessed the power of the LDP find themselves available for transforming grace. Churches will experience more than numeric growth while seeking spiritual vitality and the reserves necessary to face the forces of the post-modern world.

5

G. R. O. W. T. H. – OMEGA OPTICS

5.1 HEALTHY VISION

While much has been said in books and leadership training workshops about vision, Church vision will always include the answers to the questions; 1) How can we reach people to help connect them to Jesus and His Body? 2) In what ways will all we are doing help people grow in a healthy spiritual way? 3) What are the strategies that will encourage individuals to engage in the mission of Jesus?

The Bible teaches that *Where there is no vision, the people are unrestrained but happy is he who keeps the law.*[109] Vision comes from God and must be applied in conjunction with His commands. In formulating the vision of the church, it is important to use questions like, "What do I see the church looking like in 5 years, ten years, 25 years and when I am dead and gone?" As you describe what the "what" will look like, dream it out fully before you get caught up telling the "how." Many visions are killed by sharing the "what" too soon before the "what" is fully "baked." The leader needs to get the vision and cook it before writing the cookbook for others to follow.

RockFish Church's vision is, "to see a radically abandoned people given to the advancement of the Gospel." The "scoring" of this effort happens, "when all members are connecting relationally, growing spiritually and engaging in the cause of Christ; understanding that the Bible is the irrefutable word of God." The mission then parallels, "To build a unstoppable Church on the foundation of Jesus." As you can see, the question of "how are we going to do this?" is not fully answered. The response to this question can be practically explained by understanding how the church "scores" points for the kingdom. The practical working out of how connecting, growing, and serving is achieved will fully answer the "how" questions, but the first question to be answered is always the "what."

"Omega optics," is the idea that the "end" or "goal" of the vision needs to be fully grounded in the Scripture and God's plan for each local church as well as each person. In a world of "selfies," a selfless vision is paramount. Most people's God-given vision is never realized because life happens. Ask yourself how God would have you change your life's trajectory to accomplish His vision, then look at what you do each day. Your life consists of what you are doing each day——right now. In the light of eternity, what daily activities do you need to readjust? Ask this for your personal life and then for the ministry area you lead. Always keep in mind the end goal of the vision itself then look at the "mile markers" of your daily events to see if you are headed in the right direction. Short-term markers will help achieve the intended destination.

Understanding the complexity of RCIIH, PEPBIF, and IPNB effects will help remove unwanted roadblocks to personal as well as church-vison realization. Knowing that the Church is a living organism makes apparent that, not only are the spiritual components important, but the soulish and physical ones are as well. The view of leadership must consider the fact that Jesus died for the whole human being. He included the sanctification of the spirit, soul, and body as the package of this redemptive strategy.

> It becomes important to take into consideration the power of being transformed by mind renewal versus informational transfer.

For instance, consider the effect of the psychogenic needs[*] of the individual and

---

[*] *Psychogenic needs explain the need for power, affiliation, and achievement and its impact on influencing others.*

the effects of shame. If a shame-filled church message of the Gospel is given, shame may be the driving force behind the reason people respond the way they do. The force of shame may create a church environment that utilizes unwanted power structures along with in-groups and out-group affiliations. Shame can produce some remarkable results and achieve the pragmatic goals of the vision; however, this "short-cut" approach will not only stunt church growth, but it is also ungodly. It becomes important to take into consideration the power of being transformed by mind renewal versus informational transfer. Information transference alone may lead to unwanted spiritual illness in individuals as well as the church. Information is important, but it will not, in and of itself, accomplish the God-given vision. There are many other ways leadership may try to accomplish the vision of the church, but shame usage has to be one of the most damaging. Stated by Curt Thompson to demonstrate the root of this type of influence, "Shamed people shame people. Long before we are criticizing others, the source of that criticism has been planted, fertilized and grown in our own lives, directed at ourselves, and often in ways we are mostly unaware of."[110]

The vision of leadership is much more than creative statements and slogans pasted upon anything with a flat surface. Vision is the out-working and expression of the heart of how the leadership sees God. The vision of the church needs to be without visual obstructions. Omega Optics challenges the idea that it is possible to motivate people to do the "right thing" but with poor or dangerous methods. Pragmatic vison accomplishment is not the only goal. A healthy vision includes the achievement of the end goal within the right landscape—godliness. When the rejected disciples asked Jesus why He did not accept their performance of the "vision," He responded, "away from Me I never knew you." He stated that even though they had accomplished great and mighty works in His name, they were *workers of lawlessness*.[111]

The working out of the vision must be accomplished within the

> The working out of the vision must be accomplished within the framework of God's design.

framework of God's design.

The human experience has the capacity for great insight into the knowledge of God. God makes Himself known in a multitude of ways. The bandwidth of human involvement includes knowing God and loving Him; spirit, soul, and physicality. A precursor to having a vision of what God wants to accomplish in an individual or a church is the vision of God, Himself. Given the understanding of the interplay of RCIIH and our ability to experience Him, we can move to a vision of God that becomes transcendent of "normal" life. Apostle Paul directs us to *mind the things of the Spirit*.[112] As stated earlier, the connection point of the Holy Spirit is with our spirit as the new creature. The Bible teaches that there is a supernatural understanding and knowledge of God that is sourced in the heart. It explains that Jesus dwells in our hearts by the Holy Spirit.[113] The word "heart" here is the Greek word "kardia" meaning the literal organ of the human heart.

The human heart can know God outside of the brain's receptors of cognition. To comprehend "minding the things of the Spirit," we must understand some of the human genome makeup. By looking at the inner workings of the process of knowing and perceiving God; a greater urgency of applying the LDP will appear. I hope this understanding will lend traction to better leadership vision potential.

BRAIN

With the risk of possibly making this book too esoteric, I will include some deeper concepts of the nature of man's perceptual capacity. Keep in mind, the concept that was stated at the beginning of the book: people look to leadership/church to fulfill their expectation of the Body of Christ much the same way the characters in the Wizard of Oz approached the Emerald City. The characters in the Wizard of Oz were looking for answers to their deepest felt needs. The Scarecrow was looking for a "brain," the Tin Man was hoping for a "heart," and the Lion wanted "courage." The heroine of the story ended up acknowledging that "there is no place like home." The danger in trying to give the masses what they believe they need is the creation of a system that ends up addressing cultural felt needs leaving a church filled with only Tin Men, Scarecrows, and Fearful Lions. The challenge of church leadership is to use felt needs to bring the people the real solution to all needs which is the person of Christ. Solving the presupposed desire of the person without Christ is equivalent to building golden calves and throwing a party. The three felt needs of our yellow brick road companions demonstrate the three individual components of the human mind: the brain, heart, and cut (courage center). The mind contains the conscience and the essence of the person. Accepting the amalgamation of the mind can give insight into a person's spiritual journey and spiritual formation.

> Solving the presupposed desire of the person without Christ is equivalent to building golden calves and throwing a party.

Firstly, the mind is trans-local, meaning it does not have a specific location within the body. Secondly, the human mind is tripartite with a connection to the multilateral composition of the brain. The three main parts of the mind involve, 1) the Brain, 2) the Heart and 3) the Gut. Distortions in knowing God may occur due to some factors involving any or all of these mind dynamics. The importance of comprehending the interactions of these systems will help in the useful knowledge of the LDP.

Remember, as was just stated, the brain is not the totality of the mind, but the brain is a very important part of it. While working with the brain and its abilities to know God, it is interesting to find the parallels between the human brain and the "brain" of the church. The brain is complex in its composition. As explained by Doctor Carey,

Our brains contain one hundred billion nerve cells (neurons). Each neuron makes links with ten thousand other neurons to form an incredible three-dimensional grid. This grid therefore contains a thousand trillion connections—that's 1,000,000,000,000,000 (a quadrillion). It's hard to imagine this, so let's visualize each connection as a disc that's 1 mm thick. Stack up the quadrillion discs on top of each other, and they will reach to the sun (which is ninety-three million miles from earth) and back, three times over.[114]

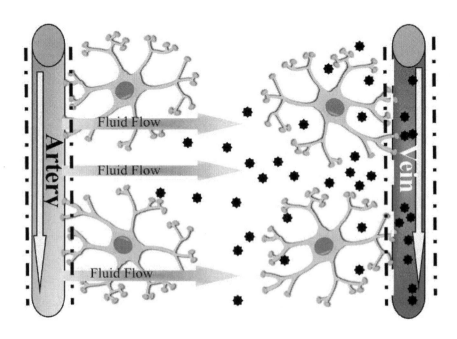

Glymphatic Cleansing System of the Brain
✳ Amyloid beta, Tau proteins, and other brain waste
Fig. 5-1

BRAIN MIND

The brain has the amazing ability to protect, control thoughts, store memories, allow for movement, regulate bodily functions, facilitate speech, hear, and see, as well as rejuvenate itself. The brain may be subdivided into three response zones — the primal "brain" (the bottom of the brain) which regulates automatic functions such as heart rate, respiratory activity, and fight or flight response (to name a few examples). The limbic "brain" perceives and gives a response to emotional situations such as danger and interpersonal input. The logic "brain" in the neocortex is responsible for handling sensory input and analytical processing.

God magnificently designed the brain. The LDP enable the brain to function properly according to His design. Excessive, prolonged stress, for example, can short-circuit the logical mechanisms and fire up the limbic response keeping it in a loop which creates a multitude of problems (such as anxiety and panic attacks). The importance of the SLDP of meditation, contemplation, and solitude come into focus. These disciplines are designed to down-regulate unnecessary physiological responses. By keeping the mind stayed upon the Lord, the mind is kept in perfect peace.

The connections of the brain are in constant flux. Some neuroscientists proclaim that approximately 35,000 brain cells die each day. Because the brain has the unique ability to conserve energy, it does its house cleaning only during the process of restorative sleep. Cleaning up the waste byproducts of the dead brain cells happens during sleep. The glymphatic system of the brain washes the brain through a complex process while many functions are suspended. God has designed mankind's brain in such a way that the brain cells "shrink" during sleep leaving greater space for the washing process to occur.

> The glymphatic system of the brain washes the brain through a complex process while many functions are suspended.

When the Restorative Sleep protocol is violated there is a buildup of leftover toxins in the brain. When this PLDP is violated over a long period, the excess toxins can cause the person to become debilitated. The key toxic substances left behind from lack of adequate sleep consists of the plaque-forming buildup of beta-amyloid and the neuron entanglement caused by Tau protein. These two are the key ingredients found in Alzheimer's and dementia. Most studies indicate a rapid, accelerated increase of these memory malfunctions in the years ahead. Projections point to as high as a 400% increase in these brain abnormalities. The PLDP of Restorative Sleep cannot be overstated. It takes the brain between seven and eight hours of sleep a night to clear these waste byproducts of neuron cell recycling. If the toxins are left uncleared, after the eleventh day without sleep, a person may die. Remember, the cleaning function of the glymphatic system of the brain only operates when a person is asleep. (See figure 5-1)

Taking care of the brain is imperative. The brain has a part in every function of the human system. The result of the Western lifestyle has not been kind to the design of the human brain. Poor nutrition (with intakes of high fructose corn syrup), lack of adequate sleep, living in a state of being overstressed, disconnection from God and others, drinking treated water (chlorine and fluoride), excess drinking of alcohol, toxic environmental exposure, violent and provocative entertainment, negativity, lack of sufficient exercise, materialism, anxiety, uncertainty, instability, main-stream philosophies of nihilism[*] and narcissistic thought all have devastating effects on the brain, as well as, the rest of the body. Researchers agree our society has a heavy price to pay if the Western culture continues in this direction. Generational epigenetic changes will impact the brain and nearly every other part of physicality, in addition to, the psychological and spiritual life of the soul.

HEART MIND

Likewise, the heart is part of the mind. The heart has neuroception[†] capabilities that interconnect with the brain to form a part of the mind that "knows the unknown." The bidirectional communication between the brain and the heart tend to co-regulate states of being. The heart consists of neurons that communicate with the brain. The heart "speaks" to the brain more than the brain speaks to the heart. The heart can "know things" outside of the awareness of the brain. The belief systems that are

---

[*] *Nihilism is the belief that life is random and is meaningless.*
[†] *Neuroception is the ability of the neural circuitry (affecting the autonomic nervous system) to evaluate risk in the environment without awareness or cognition. See the book The Polyvagal Theory by Dr. Steven Porges, (New York, New York, W.W. Norton & Company; 2017).*

sourced in the heart can refashion an individual's neuro-circuitry. Believing in nonrealities (lies) can physiologically change and damage neurons and their structures.

The heart has biophotonic* capabilities also. The light emissions of the heart adjust and change activities of the whole body and in some instances, transform the genome for future generations. The heart plays a key role in DNA epigenetic modification as well as histone modulation. The switching on and off of the DNA tags can have dramatic effects on cell structure. The heart can regulate the DNA expression. The heart controls the issues of life.[115] There are 4 million biophotonic switches in the DNA. These switches for years were known as "junk DNA" and did not have an identified purpose. Studies have demonstrated these switches are triggered through laser light-type emissions of the human heart. This process is known as neurocardial synchronization. Simply put, the heart can change the course of your life in radical ways. There is breaking research pointing towards things the Bible has already made known.

The heart also can do a threat assessment and can take over the entire bodily mechanisms, bypassing the logical brain, and preparing the body for evasive action. This automatic evaluation of risk operates with and outside of sensory input. It uses the afferent neuro pathways to communicate with the brain. The heart can affect the vagal pathway, influencing the central nervous system. According to Doctor Stephen Porges,

Safety is associated with different environmental features when defined by bodily responses versus cognitive evaluations. In a critical sense, when it comes to identifying safety from an adaptive survival perspective, the "wisdom" resides in our body and in structures of our nervous system that function outside the realm of awareness. In other words, our cognitive evaluations of

---

* *Biophotonic properties are the light emitted from the human cells that are capable of triggering the change of switches on the DNA and histones.*

risk in the environment, including identifying potentially dangerous relationships, play a secondary role to our visceral* reactions to people and places. Polyvagal Theory respects how our psychological, physical, and behavioral responses are dependent on our physiological state. The theory emphasizes the bidirectional communication between bodily organs and the brain through the vagus and other nerves involved in the regulation of the autonomic nervous system.[116]

Takotsubo cardiomyopathy (broken-heart syndrome) is an example of a perceived severe emotional loss or stress causing radical shifts in physiological states. The result can be potentially lethal. More research is beginning to uncover the importance of the heart in the neurological and genetic processes. God has designed the heart to be more than a pump. It is the entry point for spiritual connection and can change the issues of life. Guarding your heart is one of the benefits of following God's LDP. God has given the regenerated heart the ability to respond to Him, and He desires to write His design upon it.

GUT MIND

The third and final general part of the mind is the gut. Recent medical findings suggest that many neurological abnormalities originate in the gut and digestive system. Food then (as it relates to health) becomes a health deal maker or breaker. Ninety percent (90%) of all known human illnesses can be traced back to an unhealthy gut. The results of what we eat and the interplay of the gut will determine not only our health but our perception of the world. Because nutrigenomics[†] has a huge impact on DNA and gene expression, the gut's importance cannot be overstated. Food has a powerful effect down to the cellular level. DNA

Visceral: Referring to the internal organs of the body. Visceral is felt "deep down." It is the "gut feeling." Visceral reactions proceed from instinct rather than intellect.
† Nutrigenomics is the scientific study of the interaction of nutrition and genes, especially with regard to the prevention or treatment of disease.

expressional change is the reason nutrigenomics is listed as a PLDP. Put so well by Doctor Carey,

> Transgenerational effects of epigenetic changes may be one of the areas with the greatest impact on human health over the coming decades, not because of drugs or pollutants but because of food and nutrition.[117]

Many microorganisms colonize humans. Some scientists estimate that there are ten times more non-human cells in and on the body as human cells! Some of these microbes are vital to human life, and others are harmful. Within the gut, there are helpful and hurtful bacteria. These little guys not only help in the digestion of food, but they help manufacture and control serotonin. Ninety percent (90%) of serotonin is produced and regulated by the gut. Serotonin is a neurotransmitter that regulates appetite, mood, sleep and works to de-stress. Without this powerful hormone, life looks dark and depressing. Much of the symptoms of depression are the result of low or improper uptake of serotonin.

Food has a powerful influence on how we envision life. The level of health of the gut is directly correlated with the food we consume. Because of a poor diet, many health problems ensue. Too much "bad" bacteria and not enough "good" bacteria leads to a multitude of health issues. Eloquently put by Doctor David Perlmutter,

> Clearly, the good bacteria in a healthy gut are not just squatters enjoying free food and lodging. They factor into risk not just for brain disorders and mental illness but also for cancer, asthma, food allergies, metabolic conditions such as diabetes and obesity, and autoimmune disease due to their direct and indirect influences on various organs and systems. Put simply; they are in charge of your health.[118]

What we put into our mouths directly affect the microbes in our guts.

Since these microbes are bacteria, they are vulnerable to water containing chlorine and fluoride. Because good water is so important to good health, hydration is considered one of the most important PLDP. Other things like sugar, gluten, and antibiotics have a big impact on the health of the gut. High fructose corn syrup is especially damaging because the bad bacteria take this synthetic substance (along with bad fat) and creates a molecule that causes inflammation and plaque buildup in the arteries which is nearly impossible for the body to break down. High fructose corn syrup and other sugars have been shown to damage DNA, overstimulate the liver, and block the hormone that suppresses appetite. Nutrigenomics, environmental exposure, hydration, marginal management, and bodily discipline are majorly important in the PLDP designs that determine a healthy gut. IPNB and restorative sleep contribute to a healthy gut too. Interpersonal stressors and insufficient sleep can also underwrite an unhealthy gut flora.

One of the most powerful benefits is from the SLDP of self-reductionism and the discipline of fasting. Fasting not only has great spiritual connection benefits, but it also has been shown to help the natural body rest, heal, and restore. The human body has the ability to go into repair mode when a total fast[*] is implemented. It is important to note, that not everyone's body reacts the same way. It is very important for each person to "know their numbers" and approach extreme dietary changes with caution and with monitoring by a doctor. It is my opinion that everyone can and should eliminate all high fructose corn syrup, bad water, and high-fat,

> The human body has the ability to go into repair mode when a total fast is implemented.

---

[*] *A total fast consists of no food intake except for water. After 48 hours of no food the body goes into ketosis and starts the repair process. Even one or two days past the 48 hours is highly beneficial. It is not recommended for people to jump into longer fasts without a doctor's supervision. Undertaking a fast by those normally eating the standard American diet may want to transition into fasting by first eating only fruits and vegetables for a period of two weeks. This plan helps break the addictions associated with eating processed foods. Any fasting beyond 6-7 days should be done only under a physician's care.*

over-processed foods. My body seems to do best on a plant-based diet; eating approximately 20% complex carbs (bean, rice, grains, and nuts, etc.), 20% protein (Yes, plants have enough protein, but I also include organic eggs), and 60% vegetables. As stated earlier, that for the first sixty years of my life I ate anything and everything I wanted. I was a candy and sugar freak. It was due to my health that I decided to reinvent my eating habits. (see Appendix A-1). The human body is forgiving, and it will run on almost anything you give it, but eventually, poor living will take its toll. If you eat meat, eat the cleanest meat available. Limit meat intake to less than 30% of your diet. Studies have shown the gorging on meat will highly increase the risk of some cancers. I also drink the best water I can find. I want to restate that mine is not the best plan for everyone. DNA differences, seasons of life, exercise levels, and medical conditions all play an important part. The key is to eat the best food you can find and discover your unique eating profile. I do believe that in the generations ahead, due to DNA modifications form the Western lifestyle, it will become harder and harder for people not to become obese, and it will be more difficult to avoid other serious health issues. The human genome is changing, and there will be new challenges ahead in the area of bad health and diseases resulting from deviating from God's design, especially in the arena of nutrition.

Since Omega Optics is the title of this chapter, keep in mind the significance of the amalgamation of the three "brains." Poor health leads to an incorrect perception of reality. An unhealthy follower of Jesus is not as available for His purpose as a healthy one. Becoming the best "us," we can be is important in the light of being called the temple of the Holy Spirit. Following God's design for the body, soul, and spirit will enable God's people to be useful for His purposes. It is one thing to be bedridden, hospitalized, handicapped or homebound due to unavoidable sickness or unpreventable accidents; it's another thing to abuse our bodies and end up unavailable for God. We are better able to see the direction of our calling and purpose if we are not side-tracked with unnecessary health issues. A fit body, sharp mind, and a healthy spirit, God can use. Apostle Paul proclaimed it this way,

Therefore I run in such a way, as not without aim; I box in such a way, as not beating the air, but I discipline my body and make it my slave, so that, after I have preached to others, I myself will not be disqualified.[119]

Having a healthy vision, for the church and the individual in all aspects of health, needs to be taken into consideration. Seeing from God's vantage point that, physical, emotional, psychological, and spiritual readiness needs to be in place. A bad state of mind or state of being will cloud the ability to hear from God and understand the next step in life. Omega Optics is the ability to look to God without distraction or encumbrances. We will not fully be able to know God on this side of heaven but, we can attempt to hear and see His will in the best possible way. Following God's design for life makes us available and allows us the wisdom to apply and leverage His plan. As Apostle James tells us,

For if anyone is a hearer of the word, and not a doer, he is like a man who looks at his natural face in a mirror; for once he has looked at himself and gone away, he has immediately forgotten what kind of person he was. But one who looks intently at the perfect law, the law of liberty, and abides by it, not having become a forgetful hearer but an effectual doer, this man will be blessed in what he does.[120]

5.2 LOVING GOD AND OTHERS

Guiding the corporate process to the intended goal necessitates a good mission and vision statement. The end state of every vision or mission statement must hang upon the greatest commandment: loving God with everything and others like you love yourself. The "how," which was given in the teachings of Christ, gives good handles for church activities--go, make disciples, baptize, and teach all under the name and authority of Jesus. The mandate of the Savior displays the act of loving God and loving others most practically. This profound statement found in Matthew 28 may work out differently in each congregational setting, depending upon each situation, but the great command and commission directives never change. These two commands are directed to all churches. The church, as well as each life, is only successful from God's viewpoint if mission design is being followed. Test your life; test your church. How are you leading yourself and others in fulfilling this command from the Master?

STATES OF EMOTIONAL BEING

Notice that the great commandment and commission are directly pointed at relationships. It is hard to get away from the notion that the work and design of God involve others. This may sound like a very simplistic statement; however, the design of God is extremely social. The social nature of God's plan makes the understanding of why people do what they do indispensable. A lack of emotional intelligence* among leadership can have devastating consequences when it comes to the development of a healthy church. For instance, a church system or structure

> The social nature of God's plan makes the understanding of why people do what they do indispensable.

that is out of touch with the emotional state of newly arriving guests can hinder their experience from the outset of the visit. It can also be the reason people don't "stick" or become involved.

Man is a social creature. The good news is that we are a part of that human condition. Being social and having the wiring to interact with others gives us the ability to understand and have empathy for others. Doing unto others as you would have them do unto you becomes essential. As people interact, they go through emotional, physiological, psychological, spiritual, and mental states. They may not be aware of

---

Emotional Intelligence entails five different skill sets; 1) self-awareness, 2) self-regulation, 3) social skills, 4) empathy, and 5) motivation. It may be thought of as the measure of the awareness of one's emotions and the ability to grasp and navigate interpersonal relationships.

these changes, but the leadership must take these states into account. If these states are understood, it can save time, energy, resources, and relationships.

Growing in Christ includes the ability to be self-aware of these changes in states of being. As Jesus talked with the woman at the well, He was aware of changes in her as well as His own. Jesus described His change to the disciples when they questioned Him about not being hungry. Jesus was eating the whole time. The food He was eating satisfied Him the same way dinner would for someone in another state of being.[121]

A person goes through many shifts in states of being--constantly. As a new guest arrives at a church for the first time, their mind goes into the state of being of watchful safety. The need for safety is the first obligation of the mind and is never turned off. It may be turned down in a known safe environment, but it is always active. Going to a new situation tends to ramp up a reaction of apprehension. According to Doctor Porges,

> When we enter new environments, which are potentially dangerous, we shift to a surveillance vigilance system from a safe social engagement system. From a cognitive perspective, we use terms like allocation of attention. But from a neurophysiological model, it is not simply allocation of attention. We have shifted physiological state. We have reduced the neural tone to the middle ear structures so that we are better able to hear low-frequency predator sounds. But if we do that, there is an expense; we now have difficulties in hearing and understanding human voice.[122]

Awareness of this simple state of vigilance can help people involved in church guest services. Greeting people arriving for the first time at a new church requires a different approach than the person that has been coming and involved for a long period of time. Watching for primal responses* as a person arrives and adjusting the approach as necessary can go a long way in helping people adapt to the new social situation. Finding people and utilizing those that have high levels of emotional intelligence in the church is a great way to help all people feel accepted and safe.

Loving God and loving people are the greatest of commandments. Having a vision that excludes this high value of God will cloud the vision of the church and inhibit people from seeing God for the loving being He is. Understanding the magnitude of the love of God for yourself can energize your love for others. We love others from the source of being loved ourselves. The SLDP are God's strategy for helping us gain the knowledge of His love poured out upon us. We cannot love others until we know the love of God. This knowledge is supernatural. To understand the depth of His love we have to seek Him according to His ways.

5.3 A'S FOR ALL

Most people won't necessarily respond to written or commanded instructions alone. Going and reaching people in their context takes the incarnational power of Jesus working in the messenger to demonstrate loving people right where they are. Jesus almost always met the felt needs of people before He called them to correction. Every soul needs to feel His *acceptance*. God calls to "whosoever will," let them come. God's call is an open invitation into the reconciliation He paid for in full. All accounts are settled if a person responds to His offer. Outside of His offer, there is no connection, no life, no redemption, no salvation, and no hope. The Good News for everyone is that God came down and opened all the prison cells with the offer of being adopted into His care.

---

* *Primal response is the base reaction to perceived danger. The basic response of freeze, fight, flight, faint, or self-soothe can be seen in most churches on any given Sunday. One example is a slight hesitation in step as the person enters the building (this may be a fear reaction – best approach is to give them some space to adjust to the new situation before rushing in to greet with a hearty handshake)*

He has accepted all that will come out of their cell to live with Him forever! The tragedy is few take up His offer. Most stay in their cell on death row refusing to be set free and remain to trespass on a path that was made for the Devil and His crew.

Feeling accepted behind bars while being within a prison culture may appeal to some. This need for acceptance has been used to manipulate people throughout history. It is important for all human beings to feel accepted and included. Entire systems of psychology[*] have been developed that include this very important God-given need. The church offers the environment of *affiliation*. Being a place of belonging and a place of understanding should be hallmarks of the local church. The church offers acceptance of an eternal kind, and this is the greatest news ever and the best form of inclusion!

Attention is another heart cry found in every person. We all want to be known. To be heard and understood is a basic emotional need. When a person is heard, understood, and affirmed the emotional capital imparted to that individual from another person is priceless. The need to be special and cared for is common to everyone. God gave us the commission to spread the Gospel of this great power in this area. The book of Revelation is filled with the promise of being known intimately by God. The believer has been given the promise of sitting on the throne of Jesus. A new name is given that only the one receiving it will be able to hear. They receive a stone with their name on it. God will write His name directly upon the believer. God will wipe each tear away from the adopted child's eyes. The Bible also teaches that we will fully know just as we are fully known. And the follower will be just like Jesus! These together meet every cry of the heart. These needs include *admiration, appreciation, approval, affection, achievement, and advocacy* which are the longings of the heart. If God is for us who or what else matters? This Gospel optic needs to be celebrated with all.

The message of the church needs to include the power of the Gospel

---

[*] *Example - Henry Murray's Psychogenic Needs used to describe universal needs of all human beings. The three psychogenic needs are 1) need for power, 2) need of affiliation, and 3) the need for achievement.*

that fulfills these longings of the human heart. How will anyone escape if the salvation of this magnitude is neglected? The vision of every church and personal vision of each person must include the addressing of these basic felt needs and must be used according to their God-intended purpose. Gaining these heart needs and having them met outside of Christ may lead a person in a co-dependent, unhealthy, and destructive direction. The church leadership must be cautious of using these universal human needs for maneuvering people into doing even good things for the church. The exploitation and manipulation of the heart have no place in the kingdom of God. Knowing the desires of the heart and applying God's design to meet them will result in seeing Christ build His church. Seeing Jesus and His heart for His people is the outflow of Omega Optics.

5.4 VERTICAL AND HORIZONTAL CONNECTIONS

Studies demonstrate that the people you spend time with effects the longevity of your life. The connection is not just about hanging out with friends. The connection is a multifaceted need of the human design. Key studies in sociogenomics* have determined a link between adverse social interactions and inflammation, cancer, alteration in the genome, the

> The strategy of every local church should include a plan to foster and maintain good vertical and horizontal connectivity.

longevity of life, and mental health. Social interaction can enhance or inhibit the physical health of human beings. We are made to connect, and these connections can be positive or negative, with consequences on many different levels. God intended for us to attach. Spiritual health is directly related to a person's ability to connect with God and others. Church growth is predicated upon its ability to form strong, healthy connections. The strategy of every local church should include a plan to

---

* Sociogenomics looks at how social factors affect the genome and its expression.

foster and maintain good vertical and horizontal connectivity. How well a church can network people together and maintain a strong focus upon the Father will determine the level of maturity and vitality of the Body of Christ.

The ability to recognize breaks in healthy connections and the repair of breaches is everyone's responsibility. The Bible gives direct commands of how to accomplish good relationships. Matthew 5 and Matthew 18 are great chapters discussing how and when to fix broken connections. The church leadership has a unique job when it comes to maintaining the unity of the church. Relationship reconciliation is everyone's commanded obligation. As stated earlier, unity is such a high priority because it is there God commands the three-fold blessing. Body ministry by design only works appropriately when each part is operating according to God's precepts. Connectivity is one of the key SLDP. Good connectivity with people in healthy relationships and with God will have an enormous impact on the effectiveness of the local church. Connectivity along with contemplation has a direct power to help people move in empathy and compassion.

The vertical aspect of worshiping God and receiving His life is clearly stated as a top priority in the Scriptures. There needs to be a distinction between "praying" and connecting to God. Genuine prayer is a connection, but far too often "prayer" is used as a mechanistic duty that somehow religiously aligns the person to receive God's favor. Mechanized prayer is not a connection to God; this is a man-made religion. Most cultures have some form of "praying," but real prayer is two-way communion with God that is only accomplished through the purchased right of Jesus Christ. All people sense the need to unite to a higher power because God created us with the potentiality to attach to Him; however, until a person is made alive through the power of the Gospel, there is not life-giving flow.

Scientists have also found that we are "hard-wired" to connect to God. Rob Moll says,

Any kind of learning, and any kind of concentration, will cause the brain to change in response. But religious and spiritual contemplation changes your brain in a profoundly different way because it strengthens a unique neural circuit that specifically enhances social awareness and empathy while subduing destructive feelings and emotions.[123]

Although research has shown that we are "hard-wired" for connection to God, relationship with the True God is not automatic. The brain is a very conservative organ and only does what it needs to or is trained to do. Again, Moll says,

When we pray, study, meditate on Scripture, we focus our attention, and we slowly develop our ability to connect with God. Many people find prayer and contemplation methods to be hard. We sit down to pray, and nothing happens. We try to find God, but He isn't there. The same is true for the stroke victim who can't use his left arm. But as he puts mental effort into the attempt, slowly he can do what was once impossible. When a woman sits down to pray and finds it impossible, that very effort, when repeated again and again, makes possible what was once impossible.[124]

Connecting people to God and others is the work of the church. Without this, the movement of the Gospel stalls. Connectivity is one of the key SLDP. Good connectivity with people in healthy relationships and with God will have an enormous impact on the effectiveness of the local church. Remember, connectivity, along with contemplation, has a direct power to help people move in empathy and compassion.

Onlookers may disagree with the church's teaching, but they should marvel at how well the church members love each another. The care for one another and the value placed upon each part being edified should be like a dinner bell ringing that heralds the reality of the life found in Jesus. The Church, as well as each life, is called and originally designed to love God and others. Sin has broken this relationship which Jesus died to reconnect. The Holy Spirit was given to guide the believer into all truth. The Holy Spirit is the direct power to help the follower connect with God and others and to contemplate the greatness of God while growing in spiritual vitality. Guarding times of contemplation will enhance the Christian's ability to properly connect with others, causing unity, and spiritual maturity across the local church. Seeing God with eyes of loving awe is Omega Optics.

6

G. R. O. W. T. H. –
WORSHIP WONDERS

6.1 HEALTHY HEART

Then the Lord said, *"Because this people draw near with their words and honor Me with their lip service, but they remove their hearts far from Me, and their reverence for Me consists of traditions learned by rote, therefore behold, I will once again deal marvelously with this people, wondrously marvelous; and the wisdom of their wise men shall perish, and the discernment of their discerning men shall be concealed."*
Isaiah 29:13-14

God seeks worshipers that will worship in spirit and truth. Worshiping this way sounds like a simple concept; however, the fulfillment of moving into the realm of worship designed by God entails harmony of heart, mind, soul, and physicality. As described earlier, the effect of the complex nature of RCIIH (Reciprocal Cybernetic Inductional Interaction Hypothesis) explains the interaction of energies between the brain, heart, soul, spirit, and body, and allows us a base to understand the spiritual and physiological need and function of worship. All humans are wired to worship something. We were designed to seek the force outside of ourselves and pay homage to it. Our being understands the desperate requirement to connect to this force. When a person comes to Jesus Christ, the truth of this connection becomes clear. Only then, after a person has been made alive by the Spirit of God, by becoming a new creature, can he truly worship the Creator.

Loving God through worship with everything means to be integrated body, soul, and spirit—devoted totally to Him. Worshiping God with everything is what Jesus meant when He told the Samaritan woman that worship must be done in spirit and truth. Actions, thoughts, essence, and spirit are drawn into worship holistically. Logic, traditions, and thinking can all help in the worship of God, but true worship is a surrender of the total self to this moment. Focused attention of one's entire being is needed to worship God. Completeness of true worship happens when there is a synchronization of Holistic Energetic Coherence (HEC).[*] As the Holy Spirit leads through the new spirit creature, and the soul comes in harmony along with the physical energies of the body, there is a connection with God that is transcendent.

> As the Holy Spirit leads through the new spirit creature, and the soul comes in harmony along with the physical energies of the body, there is a connection with God that is transcendent.

Conversely, when the body is just going through the motions of worship (even if the words spoken are honoring God), but the heart is out of sync, this type of worship dishonors Jesus. We honor God when all the energies of our life system are online and synchronized. It is only through the design of the LDP that the worshiper can fully worship God the way He is worthy to be worshiped. The key worship protocol then becomes self-reductionism. We are to become living sacrifices.

Employing the LDP allows the follower the power to reduce self to such a degree that the connection with the Savior in worship is almost spontaneous. A lifestyle of worship allows the believer to move in and out of worship throughout the day. Because the PLDP help minimize earthly distractions and sideways energy, this gives the follower a way to mind the things of the spirit. Remember, this way of living is not adding more things to do, it is the reduction of the things that inhibit life

---

[*] *Holistic Energetic Coherence (HEC) is the optimum energy output from all of the systems related to RCIIH. When HEC's are in sync complete worship of God is in spirit and truth.*

with God. The SLDP give the heart and soul the power of alignment with the Creator which makes the heart and soul work as designed. The SLDP are not to be seen as in conflict with PLDP but are to work together to sync the whole being. The link between the physical and spiritual are not like two diametrically opposing forces but are to be viewed as having the design which allows the flesh to become subservient to the things of the spirit. A life lived out holistically, body, soul, and spirit, is the proper way God planned for Christians to function. A clear Scriptural picture of this foundation is found in 2 Corinthians 3 where it states,

> *You are a letter, written in our hearts, knowing and read by all men; being manifested that you are a letter of Christ, cared for by us, written not with ink, but with the Spirit of the living God, not on tablets of stone, but on tablets of human hearts.*[125]

To demonstrate the interplay of the physical body attributes with physiological states, that include the heart and its functioning, let's turn for a moment and see what Doctor Porges has discovered in his research,

Polyvagal Theory interprets singing as a neural exercise of the social engagement system.* Singing requires slow exhalations while controlling the muscles of the face and head to produce the modulated vocalizations that we recognize as vocal music. The slow exhalations calm autonomic state by increasing the impact of ventral vagal pathways on the heart. During the exhalation phase of breathing, vagal motor fibers send an inhibitory signal (i.e., vagal brake) to the heart's pacemaker that slows heart rate. During the inhalation phase of breathing the vagal influence to the heart is diminished and heart rate increases. Singing requires longer exhalations relative to inhalations, which

---

* *Social engagement system connects the heart with the muscles of the face and head. There is a direct correlation between the two through the somatomotor component pathways of the vagus system.*

promotes a vagal mediated calm physiological state. The process of singing couples the exercise of turning on and off the 'vagal brake' with the exercise of the neural regulation of the muscles of the face and head, including facial muscles, middle ear muscles for listening, and muscles of the larynx and pharynx for vocal intonation. Thus, singing provides an opportunity to exercise the entire integrated social engagement system.[126]

Singing during times of personal and corporate worship can have a multidimensional effect on the follower. It is important to note that, although worship can help with a physiological peace of mind, this is NOT the purpose of singing to the Lord. I use this example to demonstrate how one of the activities of worship is interconnected with the total person. The converse scenario is also true. Being overstressed, distracted, and unengaged while doing the activities

> Being overstressed, distracted, and unengaged while doing the activities of worship make a person unavailable to God.

of worship make a person unavailable to God. Using the LDP helps keep the total person positioned to connect with God and others.

The harmonics of the body, soul, and spirit can only come into the originally designed purpose if the whole is submitted to the commands of God. True worship of God flows from the integration of the whole being from the spirit to logic (truth). Accomplishing integrated worship requires the divine order. God is the author and orchestrator of true worship.

Some would have us "follow our hearts"; others would suggest that we must remain trusting in our logic; still others believe we should follow "our gut." Scripture makes known to us that none of these choices will lead us to the true reality. The unregenerate heart, for example, is the most misleading thing on earth,

The heart is more deceitful than all else and is desperately sick; who can understand it? I, the Lord, search the heart, I test the

mind, even to give to each man according to his ways, according to the results of his deeds.[127]

The harmony of all parts; the innermost being, heart, lower brain, upper brain, the right brain, and the left brain, unify to bring physical/spiritual worship to God. Integration doesn't happen only in a moment but is intended to be a lifestyle priority. One of the clearest Scriptures that includes a great mystery of this integration is found in 1 Corinthians 4:5-6. It states,

And if our Gospel is veiled, it is veiled to those who are perishing, in whose case the god of this world has blinded the minds of the unbelieving, that they might not see the light of the Gospel of the glory of Christ, who is the image of God. For we do not preach ourselves but Christ Jesus as Lord, and ourselves as your bond-servants for Jesus sake. For God, who said, "light shall shine out of darkness," is the One who has shone in our hearts to give the light of the knowledge of the glory of God in the face of Christ.

Here, contained in this passage, are the mechanisms of the interplay of the body, soul, and spirit working out under the direction of Father God. This mystery of how biochemistry and the interaction of the soul components are seen through biophotonics, epigenetic switching, histone modulation, and interpersonal neurobiology. The Gospel is the trigger of holistic worship. Understanding this harmony allows for the view of how the soul, when it yields to the Holy Spirit brings glory to God. The details of this interaction from the Holy Spirit through the entire human experience is complex and cannot be unpacked in this limited space.

The point here is that as scientists and experts stumble through the physicality of man, they inadvertently find the truth about the heart, mind, soul, and body that has been proclaimed through the Scripture for ages.

The point here is that as scientists and experts stumble through the physicality of man, they inadvertently find the truth about the heart, mind, soul, and body that has been proclaimed through the Scripture for ages. The passage we just read from 1 Corinthians Chapter 4 gives us insight into the magnificent design of God. It speaks of the "light shown in our hearts." It wasn't until recently that studies have concluded the biophotonic capabilities of the heart. This passage also talks about "the light of the knowledge of God in the face of Jesus." As we have seen the IPNB nature of man, face plays an important part in the connection of the heart. Nonverbal expression is a major part of the language of interpersonal neurobiology. Studies have shown how the facial muscles can be used to downregulate physiological states. In counseling, I have taught people how to come out of a panic or anxiety attack by simply speaking out loud to the heart in reassuring terms that everything is ok and by simply activating the muscles used for true smiling--this brings the heart back into rhythm. I have used this myself when I experience a panic attack during an extremely stressful time.

Giving some more insight into the functionality of the heart I quote Doctor Catherine Athans,

It was recently discovered that this Heart Brain has its network of forty thousand neurons. It has its perceptions. Additionally, it has its processing capacities-a hormone factory-where it is actually able to produce adrenaline and other vital hormones. It works like a conductor: it synchronizes all biological rhythms in the human being." She goes on to list some incredible functions. "It adapts its behavior according to its perceptions. It creates its own memories and uses its experiences to choose its responses. It has a small hormone factory. It produces its own adrenaline; releases ANF (atrial natriuretic factor) which regulates blood pleasure; secretes oxytocin (uses when the mother breastfeeds, during courtship, intercourse, etc.); has a close connection with the brain in the head through the vagus nerve and the nerves in the spinal column.[128]

The heart is connected directly to the facial muscles which are a factor in IPNB. It is in the face of Jesus we see the nature and glory of God. This connection has great spiritual significance to the mind/body interplay.

In the book, the Wizard of Oz, our four companions must each face the Great and Terrible Oz alone. Dorothy is first and encounters an enormous head without arms or legs. Secondly, the Scarecrow sees Oz as a lovely lady. The Tinman, in turn, beholds a beast that resembles a rhinoceros with five eyes, five arms, and five legs. Lastly, the Cowardly Lion enters the throne room of the Great One and perceives a ball of fire. As people engage the local church, sooner or later they will encounter the "facial" effects of the governmental leadership in the church. Their expectations of leadership may result in the same reactions as those of the Oz characters.

As Dorothy and her band returned from encountering the Great and Powerful Oz, they all experienced feelings of surprise, disappointment, sorrow, and anger. Likewise, these feelings are not uncommon in the church setting. Incorrect expectations on leadership, or misperception of their role, often causes stress and disappointment. Not only can this false reality short-circuit a good relationship towards leadership, but the self-perception of individuals can also bring about difficulty. In the story of Oz, the group of travelers saw themselves as "helpless," "deficient," and "powerless." Remember that the psychogenic needs of a person explain the need for power (Lion's courage), affiliation (Dorothy's home—Tinman's heart), and achievement (Scarecrow's brains). When a person believes that they are deficient in one of these areas, they sense an intrinsic weakness in themselves. These lies of inadequacies have the impact of circumventing the power of the believer. As in the story of the Wizard of Oz, the cohorts had all the power they needed to have great thoughts, operate with big hearts, experience fearless courage, and return home. The same way Dorothy and her friends were looking to a man to fix their problems, people in the church can expect the leadership to solve theirs. Jesus is all anyone needs. The Leadership's job is to point to Him and encourage the congregation to connect directly to God. God has given the follower the "Gospel shoes" that have all the power to destroy the enemies of God and take them home. Leaders are merely guides showing the way to the Life Force: God. This type of worship will encourage true worship.

Leaders that try to assume the position of the Great and Powerful Oz will surely lead the people they guide into disillusionment and codependency. The power for life transformation is resident in the true believer. The follower wears the Gospel shoes and will soon crush the enemy with them. Leaders are to underscore this reality and lead people into worship wonders.

6.2 HEART LIVING AT THE FEET OF JESUS

It is important to note that even with research developments and new technological advancements, the best way to come to God is as a child. We should all remember that *unless you are converted and become like children, you will not enter the kingdom of heaven.*[129] Jesus was not saying to throw out your brain and pretend. He is speaking about trust. By nature, children are generally trusting to authority figures and have not developed the cynicism brought about by life's letdowns.

The balance to this idea is found in a statement made by Apostle Paul when he says, *put away childish things.*[130] At first hearing, this seems to contradict the teachings of Christ. But, when it comes to growing up to be like Christ, the fantasy nature given to children (that protects their minds from trauma) breaks down as the mind fully develops. The adult can no longer rely on this God-given mechanism after the age of about 26—about age 26 the brain is fully matured. Fantasy was given to the limbic brain of a child as a prime directive for survival. If this mechanism is allowed to continue into adulthood as an escape device, it turns into believing lies as a coping mechanism. The call of God is to speak the truth in the inner man. As we mature into adulthood, it is imperative to remain trusting as a child without creating false realities.

By sitting at the feet of Jesus in undistracted adoration, the result is the sustaining, healing, and restoring of even the most broken soul. A healthy spiritual person becomes free to decrease and let Jesus increase resulting in true worship. A lifestyle of daily dependence will not only bring glory to God through worship but will also heal the worshiper.

The things that crowd out this relationship with Jesus will also choke out spiritual maturity. Distractions of the modern world and fast-paced living leaves the follower empty and unfruitful. Maintaining good SLDP keep the worship fresh and real. The practices of solitude, meditation, connectivity, Sabbath observation, and spiritual contemplation all help open up the soul to the healing and maturing factors that are given by the Holy Spirit. These disciplines are designed to dispel deeply embedded lies, filling the soul with strength and encouragement. We must sit with Jesus continually and soak in His presence, while attentive to His Word. Healthy growth for the church is assured if the followers of Jesus grow in their worship and adoration of the Master.

> Healthy growth for the church is assured if the followers of Jesus grow in their worship and adoration of the Master.

6.3 ATMOSPHERE OF VIRTUE

As the corporate body of believers assemble, having a unified, healthy, spiritual atmosphere is critical if the Holy Spirit is to bless. God eagerly awaits us when we gather in His name. "Gather" is a powerful concept. It means to join as one. Unity is where God commands a blessing. Conversely, entering God's realm of joint worship while in disunity is a stench in the nostrils of God and profanes the sacrifice for which Jesus paid such a high price. Even in the Lord's prayer, Jesus makes clear the reality that if we decide to move in disunity and broken connections, the Father will disconnect also. Jesus said that *if you do not forgive men their transgressions, your heavenly Father will not forgive your transgressions.*[131] (Unforgiveness blocks the grace of God).

Forgiveness is one of the most important virtues in creating an atmosphere of worship. This form of humility allows for strength to flow in and through the Body of Christ. It is recorded in the Old Testament that, *O Lord, Thou hast heard the desire of the humble; Thou wilt strengthen their heart, Thou wilt incline Thine ear.*[132] Nothing brings people closer to God jointly than authentic vulnerability. Humility unlocks the pathway into His realm. Gratitude opens the gates while giving Him glory puts the people into the courts of the Lord.[133] Likewise, a fully functioning follower will exhibit one of the most God-like qualities known as extreme generosity termed munificence. Munificence is one of the SLDP and is only developed as the believer is moving in true self-reductionism. One of the aspects of God's glory is munificence. When God gave the Ten Commandments, He demonstrated His nature as a giving God.

> One of the aspects of God's glory is munificence.

The fact that He gave one of the commandments as a gift to mankind[134] should give all of us the reaction of spontaneous praise. The Sabbath was made as a gift to man. Not just the idea of taking a day off, but He showed us our design and the need to reconnect to The Creator for spiritual recharging. He knew we would need this gift as humanity has ADD (Always Doing Different) things than the design. He gave us the breadcrumbs of life that lead us back to reconnection with Him. In His munificence, He gave us Himself. He made Himself available to us! Making ourselves available to God and His purposes also make us extravagant in our availability to others. The result of the LDP is availability. When God's people metabolize the virtues of wisdom, grace, hope, empathy, along with gratitude, humility, forgiveness, and munificence, heaven will come down to bless with true spiritual growth. The world needs to see more of this true expression of worship among God's people. Imagine.

7

G. R. O. W. T̲. H. –
THEOCRATIC TAPESTRY

7.1 HEALTHY BONES

As physical bones hold the natural body upright; the spiritual bones give the Body of Christ structure to operate. How a church is structured will regulate the course of growth, its connection points, and its directional movement. If church structure is strong and healthy, the rest of the Body will reflect health. In contrast, a poor structure will hinder growth and productivity—and worse still— poor structure causes damage to the rest of the Body of Christ. The tapestry of interwoven forces within the church and the correlation of individual and community experience is stabilized by the Bible mandated structure of the theocracy.

In speaking about how power and authority are disseminated to a group of people, we are talking about government. Whether we are talking about a monarchy, patriarchy, oligarchy, matriarchy, communism, democracy, republic, socialism, or parliamentary structures, the purpose is the same--movement of power and authority toward a group of people. There are many ways to form a government in the natural sense. All societies have some form of government. However, good government empowers, protects, and facilitates good growth for the people under its influence while poor government leads to destruction, neglect, or abuse.

Good structure promotes unity in the church. Unity is the good soil that leads to healthy church growth, and in turn, also helps individuals grow and mature. For this reason, church government is important for church growth. The book of Ephesians states,

He gave some as apostles, and some as prophets, and some as evangelists, and some as pastors and teachers, for the equipping of the saints for the work of service, to the building up of the Body of Christ; until we all attain to the unity of the faith, and of the knowledge of the Son of God, to a mature man, to the measure of the stature which belongs to the fullness of Christ.[135]

The direction of spiritual maturity is always pointed toward Christ; to be like Him. Remember, unity is the good soil that leads to healthy growth. A good structure promotes unity and deals with conflict.

The Old Testament Hebrew children were to be structured governmentally as a theocracy. It was God's design for the Hebrews to have Him as their king. They were to take His commands and structure into every area of their lives accordingly. They were to live by His Word. God designed their social, judicial, civil, cultural, and religious laws as a unit for them to follow. They were to be different in every way from the rest of the people of the world. Specific instructions were given for every part of the Hebrew life. The way they wore their hair, adorned their bodies, conducted business, handled unruly children, ate their meals, facilitated inheritance, worshiped, married, divorced, steered criminal trials, took care of accidents, dealt with foreigners, made clothes, cooked their food, and about any other area of life imaginable were included in God's laws. In total, nine books of the Old Testament detailed these mandates.

With God as their king and all the laws in place, the only thing needed was the dispensing of the laws to the people—law enforcement. God commanded that judges determine how to apply the laws to any given situation. They were not to write the laws but interpret them and oversee their application. The book of Judges shows this action in motion. It wasn't long until the Children of Israel demanded a king like the rest of the nations around them. They wanted to give up the kingship of heaven for the earthly counterfeit. Most of the rest of the history of

Israel is related to whether the king was godly or not. The spiritual connection of the earthly king with God determined the national state of Israel.

The understanding of this dynamic will help in the study of Old Testament truths. Trying to apply the totality of Israel's laws to the church today would prove to be devastating. Understanding this will help see why God had rebellious children stoned to death or how Elisha the prophet could justify calling bears out of the woods to eat kids; it was the law, and the punishment was prescriptive. A lack of understanding of how the grace of God in Christ has birthed the Church into a new place will confuse. All the law is now based upon the finished work of Jesus. *Jesus is the end of the law for righteousness to everyone who believes.*[136] Every point of the law is fulfilled in Christ perfectly. No more sacrifices for sin, not cutting the sides of the hair, killing children that are rebellious etc., Jesus completely fulfilled every jot and tittle of the law.

When considering how to construct church government from the philosophy of the Old Testament pattern, it is important always to allow the New Testament to interpret the Old. The New Testament is the full revelation of God's plan and design. Upon consideration of the many possible ways to organize church government for RockFish Church, we wanted to get it right. We were not looking for the most pragmatic or traditional church answers of how to form the bone structure of the church. We looked to the New Testament pattern and discovered that Apostle Paul structured churches following the theocratic model. As Paul traveled proclaiming the Gospel, churches were formed. These tiny groups of followers needed to have direction and teaching. They needed government.

Paul lays out the pattern that can be seen in the Scripture as he sets in a new pastor with the theocratic instructions. He instructs young Timothy,

Now to the King eternal, immortal, invisible, the only God, be honor and glory for ever and ever. Amen. Timothy, my son, I am

giving you this command in keeping with the prophecies once made about you, so that by recalling them you may fight the battle well, holding on to faith and a good conscience, which some have rejected and so have suffered shipwreck with regard to the faith. Among them are Hymenaeus and Alexander, whom I have handed over to Satan to be taught not to blaspheme. First of all, then, I urge that entreaties and prayers, petitions and thanksgivings, be made on behalf of all men, for kings and all who are in authority, so that we may lead a tranquil and quiet life in all godliness and dignity. This is good and acceptable in the sight of God our Savior, who desires all men to be saved and to come to the knowledge of the truth. For there is one God, and one mediator also between God and men, the man Christ Jesus, who gave Himself as a ransom for all, the testimony given at the proper time. For this I was appointed a preacher and an apostle (I am telling the truth, I am not lying) as a teacher of the Gentiles in faith and truth. Therefore, I want the men in every place to pray, lifting up holy hands, without wrath and dissension. Likewise, I want women to adorn themselves with proper clothing, modestly and discreetly, not with braided hair and gold or pearls or costly garments, but rather by means of good works, as is proper for women making a claim to godliness. A woman must quietly receive instruction with entire submissiveness. But I do not allow a woman to teach or exercise authority over a man, but to remain quiet. For it was Adam who was first created, and then Eve. And it was not Adam who was deceived, but the woman being deceived, fell into transgression. But women will be preserved through the bearing of children if they continue in faith and love and sanctity with self-restraint. It is a trustworthy statement: if any man aspires to the office of overseer, it is a fine work he desires to do. An overseer, then, must be above reproach, the husband of one wife, temperate, prudent, respectable, hospitable, able to teach, not addicted to wine or pugnacious, but gentle, peaceable, free from the love of money. He must be one who manages his own household well, keeping his children under control with all dignity (but if a man does not know how to manage his own household, how will he take care of the church of God?), and not a new convert, so that he will not become conceited and fall into the condemnation incurred by the devil. And he must have a good reputation with those outside the church, so that he will not fall into reproach and the snare of the devil. Deacons likewise must be men of dignity, not double-tongued, or addicted to much wine or fond of sordid gain but holding to the mystery of the faith with a clear conscience. These men must also first be tested; then let them serve as deacons if they are beyond reproach. Women must likewise be dignified, not malicious gossips, but temperate, faithful in all things. Deacons must be husbands of only one wife, and good managers of their children and their own households. For those who have served well as deacons obtain for themselves a high standing and great confidence in the faith that is in Christ Jesus.[137]

Paul continues,

Let no one look down on your youthfulness, but rather in speech, conduct, love, faith, and purity, show yourself an example of those who believe. Until I come, give attention to the public reading of the Scriptures, to exhortation and teaching. Do not neglect the spiritual gift within you, which was bestowed upon you through prophetic utterance with the laying on of hands by the presbytery.[138]

RockFish Church adopted this church government model of the New Testament Theocracy. The Senior Pastor acts as the leader conducting the meetings of the Board of Elders with the Deacons in attendance. The Elder and Deacon members are permanent, called positions. The Lead or Senior Pastor sets the vision of the church and the Elder

Board determines the timing and confirmation, all the while lining up everything against God's Holy Word and His vision for the church.

The Board has changed in practical function as RockFish Church grew over the years. In the early days, the pastor, elders, and deacons did most of the week to week work. Their hands were in everything. Day-to-day operational tasks were done primarily by the pastor. As the congregation grew, the leadership still had their hands in everything, but others were raised up to take on the tasks. The church at this size was nearing the 200-attendance mark. In the latter years, it has become necessary for the Governmental Leadership Board to transition to mostly teaching, preaching, policy-making and pastoring-type activities. It was necessary for the growth of the church to move to each phase of functioning at the right time. Proper growth will be hampered if the leader does not recognize these seasons of church governance.

Having the right people in the right position forms the structural support for healthy growth. Conversely, the wrong person may stop or impede the healthy growth process. Each person has a limit of effectiveness. Seasons in any organization must be capitalized, taken into account, and leveraged. Jesus taught and lived out the strategy of releasing power, authority, responsibility, and consequences to His disciples. He left them to carry on the task of the ministry. He said it was for their benefit that He was to leave. He told them that they would accomplish more than He did. As leaders, we must become masters of giving the needed amount of power and authority away at the correct season and having the right people in the right spots at the precise time. I believe this to be one of the greatest structural attributes for healthy growth. In Dr. Henry Cloud's book, *Necessary Endings*, Henry lays out this important principle. He states,

> Rosebushes and other plants produce more buds than the plant can sustain. The plant has enough life and resources to feed and

nurture only so many buds to their full potential; it can't bring all of them to full bloom. In order for the bush to thrive, a certain number of buds have to go. The caretaker constantly examines the bush to see which buds are worthy of the plant's limited fuel and support and cuts the others away. He prunes them. Takes them away, never to return. He ends their role in the life of the bush and puts an end to the bush's having to divert resources to them.[139]

When applying this to church structure, it becomes clear that the "pruning" away of the vast array of activities by the leadership is essential. The leadership must maintain focus on the most productive use of energy. I highly recommend Dr. Clouds book on this subject and its application to both personal and church life. The transitions of focused activity by the leadership can hinder or advance the growth of the church. Recognizing the growth hindrances of holding on too tightly in the areas of control and power is the duty of the senior leaders. I realize that removing direct contact in areas of ministry can be a frightening endeavor. It is, however, critical for the advancement of God's kingdom. It is also exciting and fulfilling seeing a disciple grow and become a fruitful leader. This culture of releasing people into their calling and knowing how to develop them creates a sustainable structure where every "joint supplies." The parts working together will allow for sustained healthy growth, an abundance of people engaged in serving, and a functional way to develop an unending supply of leaders.

7.2 PERSON

Every individual must allow the Holy Scriptures to scrutinize their entire life to see if their life is being governed by the precepts of God. Individual spiritual health will allow for Christian maturity. Learning the necessity of submission, self-control, yielding, and reduction of individualism by reading and incarnating God's Word becomes the lifeblood of a strong walk with Jesus. Using the SLDP to feed on the life of Christ becomes imperative. Personal rights, responsibilities, and consequences fall into place as the disciple follows the teachings of Jesus. The governance of the Bible in every area is not only encouraged but expected. Jesus calls us to walk as He did. For the Body of Christ to effectively move forward, there is no place for the follower to pick and choose what commands he/she will obey. The theocracy of God mandates full compliance. The individual opinion of what constitutes relevance of right and wrong must always submit to God's design.

7.3 FAMILY

As stated earlier, the qualifications of an elder include proper family order. Healthy family functioning under the direction of God's instruction is the platform for all godly ministry. If this important foundational platform is not solid, this weakness will seep into the ministry. The leader's ability to lead or not is seen in the discipleship of the home. Society and churches are built upon the family unit. God-ordained family systems are critical to the health of the local church. Prioritizing family will not automatically assure that every member of all families will follow Jesus or will be without problems, but the handling of the issues as they arise will demonstrate the leadership influence and effectiveness in the home. When it comes to spiritual health, the priority of leadership is established in the home.

> When it comes to spiritual health, the priority of leadership is established in the home.

The most dangerous effect of living two distinct expressions of faith is manifested in the home. Hypocrisy carries with it the most damaging consequences to the subsequent generations. Children will value or devalue what is modeled in front of them. Never underestimate or overlook the significance of parental influence upon children in the home. Children develop best in a safe, affirming, valuing, and hope-giving environment. Helping the kids find their purpose will also help them learn how to use power throughout their lives. Proper development includes spiritual safety, God's designed purpose, eternal value, and long-lasting hope. The responsibility of imparting these ingredients falls upon both parents. The proper working of the multifaceted influences in the home will keep improper power shifts from derailing unity.

7.4 CHURCH

There are many different setups used to disperse power within a church and understanding the powers and influencers of a church is critical. It is important to always link power, responsibility, and consequences when forming boundaries that will keep the structure interdependent and not co-dependent or independent. The question of "who has the God-given power to make the needed change?" must be put together with responsibility and accountability. A person with the true power to make change must take responsibility for the outcome. A title alone does not constitute this position. Major problems may arise if incorrect anticipations or assumptions are held. Clear values, expectations, and roles must be understood by all involved.

Problems will always be a part of every church, but the way things are handled will determine the spiritual well-being of the Body. While many pastors have inherited poor governmental structures, it does not matter the strategies, titles, vision, or plans of the past if the structure of the leadership is not a theocracy. There are many different setups to disperse power within a church and understanding the powers and influencers of a church is critical. It is a sad commentary when people with this power usurp God's design, and if the structure is not well established, the church will suffer greatly. A theocratic church form of government will protect the church from an undercurrent of disunity. At RockFish Church, I am blessed to have a well-founded system of government based upon the Word of Truth that helps guide and protect the Body.

There is an atmosphere at RockFish that feels safe. Safe to try. Safe to fail. Safe to connect and to disconnect. People see the leadership as active and caring. Ministry is shared, and power is given to others allowing for a broad platform of service delivery. There is a baptism culture where all those in leadership take part in offering baptism. Seeing dads baptize their families sends one of the loudest messages to onlookers. Permission granting and empowerment gives the church members a feeling of ownership.

At RockFish Church, I am blessed to have a theocracy that helps guide and protect the Body. When problems arise, the answers are found in Scripture; not political prowess. It is a blessing to have this safety net and the quality of leaders I have the honor of serving alongside. We have, at times disagreed but the hurt experienced has not been harmful. Spiritual growth in the church can come through pain, but hurt many times leads to growth. Maintaining a culture of Christian virtue and handling each heart as precious has led to strong sustained growth.

Most of the difficulties over the years have been due to the same things many marriages discover. Failed expectations, differing values, individual perceptions, confused roles, and of course, lies of the enemy are the sources of many of the snags. As in all relationships, communication with clarity reduces the stress of these glitches. Another key is keeping mutual respect and trust at the top of the list. This priority helps keep these problems from becoming real issues. Churches will always have situations that cause complications but having a theocratic mindset allows for resolutions that strengthen the spiritual life of the Body.

8

G. R. O. W. T. <u>H.</u> –
HEALTHY HOME (EAT YOUR "P'S")

In the home, usually, mom sets the atmosphere which sets up the cultural "feel." As followers of the Great God, we have the Holy Spirit to set the tone of our lives and the church. No plan, statement, strategy, method, approach, or government will overcome the cultural power of a church. Building the "feel" and function of the church must be done deliberately, with clarity and commitment. A church's culture will outlast any pastor. Therefore, it is important that the church is focused directly on the Gospel and teachings of Jesus. This focus on Jesus will help ensure the church's culture does not drift into the next new teaching and take emphasis away from the only true foundation.

The culture of the church can also be called the "house rules." If the expectations, values, and purposes are established and trusted, the congregation will self-correct. Teachableness and humility allow the Body to stay connected to Jesus. For example, if a self-serving attitude manifests, the Body will reject this value and correct toward a meeker posture. If pride and self-promotion are discovered, the Body will exert social energy that will point back to the teachings of Jesus.

A firm understanding of the Gospel, as well as the heart of Christ's teachings by the entire congregation, is critical. This means that the diet of the church needs to be centered around these truths. Too many directional changes in messages will lend itself toward confusion. Putting the Gospel as the prime message-driver does not mean that the messages can't include illustrations from the Old Testament or the use

Jesus has transformed us from being "sub-zeros" to "sub-heroes." Jesus is the hero.

of exegesis from any other than the Gospel writings, but what it does mean is that it should always be tied back to the real hero of the scripture; Jesus. Jesus has transformed us from being "sub-zeros" to "sub-heroes." Jesus is the hero. The Gospel is the power of God. The Gospel is our message and the hope for all lives. Jesus gave the church clear and definite instructions for her calling, and we must guard it with intentionality.

Clearly understanding the purpose of the individual as well as the corporate Body creates a purpose that empowers. Conversely, the wrong purpose will create power in the wrong direction. Defining priorities will help keep the church moving and unified on the right course. Keeping the main thing as *the main thing* will allow a place for the Holy Spirit to draw others into the mission. When the church centers around the same resolution, the people feel empowered. This unity of goal brings the blessing of God. His power is released through the Gospel, and it is the only transforming power we have that brings about healthy church growth.

8.1 POWER

The transference of the Gospel is God's power. The Gospel is transported through preaching, teaching, and the incarnational work in every believer. It is through this life transformative power that growth occurs. It does not happen through the slick presentation or the raising of the voice but through the demonstration of Christ's power. It is absurd to reduce the movement of God to our abilities and the use of man's logical persuasion. According to the Apostle James, *man's logic is natural and demonic.*[140] Building a life, a church, or a movement requires more than just knowing the purpose, it takes God's wisdom.

Wisdom is a gift that comes from God to give the builder the understanding of what principle to apply when. The resources for wisdom involve having learned many Scriptural principles. Being a student of

God's Word is necessary to bring the right principle to bear at the right time. One of the functions of the Holy Spirit is to bring thoughts to remembrance. He is the guiding force behind the application of God's wisdom. Wisdom is the power of God. God gives wisdom to those who humbly ask.

For the word of the cross is foolishness to those who are perishing, but to us who are being saved it is the power of God. For it is written, "I will destroy the wisdom of the wise, And the cleverness of the clever I will set aside." Where is the wise man? Where is the scribe? Where is the debater of this age? Has not God made foolish the wisdom of the world? For since in the wisdom of God the world through its wisdom did not come to know God, God was well-pleased through the foolishness of the message preached to save those who believe. For indeed Jews ask for signs and Greeks search for wisdom; but we preach Christ crucified, to Jews a stumbling block and to Gentiles foolishness, but to those who are the called, both Jews and Greeks, Christ the power of God and the wisdom of God.* Because the foolishness of God is wiser than men, and the weakness of God is stronger than men. For consider your calling, brethren, that there were not many wise according to the flesh, not many mighty, not many noble; but God has chosen the foolish things of the world to shame the wise, and God has chosen the weak things of the world to shame the things which are strong, and the base things of the world and the despised God has chosen, the things that are not, so that He may nullify the things that are, so that no man may boast before God. But by His doing you are in Christ Jesus, who became to us wisdom from God, and righteousness and sanctification, and redemption, so that, just as it is written, "Let him who boasts, boast in the Lord." And when I came to you, brethren, I did not come with superiority of speech

---

* *Emphasis added by author.*

or of wisdom, proclaiming to you the testimony of God. For I determined to know nothing among you except Jesus Christ, and Him crucified. I was with you in weakness and in fear and in much trembling, and my message and my preaching were not in persuasive words of wisdom, but in demonstration of the Spirit and of power, so that your faith would not rest on the wisdom of men, but on the power of God. Yet we do speak wisdom among those who are mature; a wisdom, however, not of this age nor of the rulers of this age, who are passing away; but we speak God's wisdom in a mystery, the hidden wisdom which God predestined before the ages to our glory; the wisdom which none of the rulers of this age has understood; for if they had understood it they would not have crucified the Lord of glory; but just as it is written, "Things which eye has not seen and ear has not heard, And which have not entered the heart of man, all that God has prepared for those who love Him." For to us God revealed them through the Spirit; for the Spirit searches all things, even the depths of God. For who among men knows the thoughts of a man except the spirit of the man which is in him? Even so the thoughts of God no one knows except the Spirit of God. Now we have received, not the spirit of the world, but the Spirit who is from God, so that we may know the things freely given to us by God, which things we also speak, not in words taught by human wisdom, but in those taught by the Spirit, combining spiritual thoughts with spiritual words. But a natural man does not accept the things of the Spirit of God, for they are foolishness to him; and he cannot understand them, because they are spiritually appraised. But he who is spiritual appraises all things, yet he himself is appraised by no one. For who has known the mind of the Lord, that he will instruct Him? But we have the mind of Christ.[141]

8.2 PURPOSE

In recent days, much has been said about the subject of purpose. Purpose needs to be seen in relationship to God's design. The use of purpose is powerful and lends itself to be either constructive or destructive. According to Rick Warren,

> The purpose of your life is far greater than your own personal fulfillment, your peace of mind, or even your happiness. It's far greater than your family, your career, or even your wildest dreams and ambitions. If you want to know why you were placed on this planet, you must begin with God. You were born by His purpose and for His purpose.[142]

The purpose is the driving force of the essence of a person. The reason purpose is so important is related to one's perception of their purpose. The relationship between purpose and power can be illustrated by the dynamic of the first-time social interaction of male adults. In the male world, when they meet another male, the first few verbal interactions will include the question, "so what do you do?". This question is designed to size-up one another. The higher the purpose given in this answer will characterize the male hierarchical power system. Many times, therefore doctors, engineers, helicopter pilots, and high-ranking military officers are comfortable going to social events. Conversely, trash men, ditch diggers, janitors, and low-ranking military personnel tend to be uncomfortable in unknown social engagements involving others of higher status. In the man's world, what a person does gives that person greater or less power than others. Obviously, this is an incorrect Biblical view, but none the less, this interaction surfaces. The Scripture says, *And He (Jesus) said to them, "You are those who justify yourselves in the sight of men, but God knows your hearts; for that which is highly esteemed among men is detestable in the sight of God."*[143] A high percentage of males have as their greatest fear, the fear of rejection. This fear explains many males' reactions to perceived purpose. Low purpose equates to low power in the male ego. This attention to ranking may result in the slowing of spiritual growth.

Purpose determines the positional power of a person. As a child grows up, the child determines his/her power in the world from their given purpose by others. For example, a child that grows up in a sexually abusive home will conclude that sex is their purpose. Developmental psychologists have determined that the first 15 years of a child's life will set the trajectory well into adulthood. The primary influencers in a child's life, usually the parents or some adult figure, form the child's purpose and by default, they are taught how to use this power. If the youngster is given the wrong purpose, they will grow up feeling powerless or use their given purpose to influence or manipulate others. It is essential for children to be trained up in their God-given purpose. Understanding and demonstrating power usage is one of the main responsibilities of parenting.

> Purpose determines the positional power of a person.

In counseling, the spiritual health of the person is largely shaped by the childhood imprinting of their perceived purpose. To gain the correct use of power derived from purpose, the lies sown must be replaced with the Truth. The belief structure of their purpose has a powerful influence on their spiritual growth. True freedom comes from finding an incorrect mindset and replacing it with the freedom-giving Truth. Applying life transformation and conformity to the mind of Christ is the job of those doing the discipling.

The healthy spirituality of a congregation is seen when the Body moves in their true purpose. The task of church leadership is to convey the overall purpose for the people. It is also necessary to help each part discover their purpose as it relates to the grander purpose. As every part gives their purpose to the whole, the entire Body grows in a healthy way toward the plan of God. Communicating purpose is not a onetime event. It must be overstated and taught. Creating a culture of corporate purpose will help guide the individuals. Sideways energy into incorrect expectations will only lead to division and time wasted. It is the duty of church leadership, at all levels, to monitor misleading communication. The purpose of each church must be communicated with precision to be perceived by all.

If a church's purpose is too broad, it becomes hard to visualize practically. One of the best ways to keep the applied purpose in focus is to describe the "win" for the church. When does the ministry put "points on the board"? In what way does the church score? The answer to these questions will help define the "win'. As in various sports, scoring is often different. Basketball, football, soccer, and volleyball all score differently. Helping the people understand when points count will help keep the church clear about her purpose and activities.

At RockFish Church, for example, we score when we help a person connect to the Body of Christ. It may not be exclusively connecting to RockFish, because RockFish Church is not for everyone. We try to help people plug into other churches if RockFish is not a good fit for them. For instance, they may not like the fact that our children worship as families together during the services. Or, they may not like the multicultural environment. They may not believe that a person can be a follower of Jesus and serve in the United States military. Whatever the reason, we make points if they find a church and connect. Another way we put points on the board is when a person connects to Jesus Christ. This one is obvious. We also make a score when a person grows in their relationship with Jesus. Scoring is measured in three ways; when a person, 1) loves Jesus more than before, 2) engages in a ministry, or 3) serves the Body in some capacity.

Helping people discover their God-given purpose is the work of disciple making. In evangelism, the goal is to communicate the Gospel in such a way that the person hears that their first purpose is being an object of God's affection. He wants to apply forgiveness to them and redeem them by placing them into His plan. Connecting people to God's design and helping them grow as they serve others is the job of the Body of Christ. The uniqueness of each church and God's purpose, when discovered, becomes the catalyst for healthy spiritual growth.

8.3 POSTURE

Within the church culture, there is a spiritual dimension of what I term as the "posture" of the Body of Christ. In much the same way, human body language expresses much more than words alone. The Body of Christ communicates to onlookers beyond the verbal message projected. Becoming aware of the unspoken message sent to those entering the church will help develop a coherent communication of acceptance and value. As a retired FBI agent in counterintelligence, specializing in non-verbal communication, Joe Navarro explains the importance of unspoken communication in his book,

> Nonverbal communication also reveals a person's true thoughts, feelings, and intentions. For this reason, nonverbal behaviors are sometimes referred to as tells (they tell us about the person's true state of mind). Because people are not always aware they are communicating nonverbally, body language is often more honest than an individual's verbal pronouncements, which are consciously crafted to accomplish the speaker's objectives.[144]

> The church leadership must understand the silent communication of the body they lead to have a healthy outreach growth strategy. The church gives off nonverbal cues to the arriving guests.

The church leadership must understand the silent communication of the body they lead to have a healthy outreach growth strategy. The church gives off nonverbal cues to the arriving guests. Knowing that the primal response of each person is threat assessment means that there needs to be intentional effort to lessen this effect. Going into a new experience causes apprehension. Understanding that a new person to the church is under varying degrees of anxiety, just by going to a new church, will help develop a plan to show genuine values of admiration, appreciation, approval, affection, achievement, advocacy, and acceptance. How the church is set up to communicate safety, and individual acknowledgment will go a long way in helping a guest overcome their fearful feelings. Being aware of these obstacles is the starting point and begins even before a guest arrives for the service.

8.4 PLAY BALL

In a Western cultural setting, it becomes necessary to understand underlying values that drive and influence each of us. The values, expectations, and historical baggage of living in America causes opposing energy to affect the church. Living in this environment, having an awareness of these forces, and knowing how to navigate through them will aid in keeping the church healthy. Likewise, in each person, these forces may play a role in hindering spiritual growth. When doing mission operations in a different culture, the nuisance of these structures may hinder the advancement of the Gospel. Imposing Western values upon others becomes problematic also.

One of the leading negative paradigms is the overwhelming force of individualism. In the West, we value independence and self-sufficiency. Strength is championed as the ability to stand autonomously. It is likewise important to understand that the force of co-dependency is a reactionary device caused by a culture of separation and disconnection. The Bible calls on the people of God to become interdependent and reciprocally edifying. The Body of Christ, when operating healthily, builds itself up in a mutual fashion. The parts must come together to supply purpose, unity, and growth. Individualism must be addressed for spiritual growth to take place.

Likewise, consumerism has eroded the fabric of the Christian Church in the West. This difficulty lies in the notion that the flow and direction of blessing are towards the individual. Subtly, this ingrained idea opposes the very fabric of God's design--which is based on love and giving. The picking and choosing of many options result in a perception that the individual is in the "driver's seat." The Jesus-following church must stand against the felt need to be in control and the purpose of the self-centered life.

Finding heightened ways of self-gratification through entertainment and pleasure-seeking counterfeits the true pleasure found in God Himself. A new form of Christian hedonism has developed and is being propagated into every church and home (now even further through the digital revolution). The church, as well as individual followers, must keep focused and vigilant over these matters. Healthy spiritual growth will be hindered if each of these cultural forces is not addressed effectively. The Body of Jesus must learn to function together in a mutually interdependent way. The parts, when functioning properly together, become exceptionally greater and the church grows up in her maturity through this unity.

8.5 PLACE

The saying goes, "there is a time and a place for everything." When each person finds their place and every church steps into Her place, they become an unstoppable force that advances God's Kingdom. It then becomes the job of the church to develop an executable plan that addresses this need. Having a way to help each follower discover more of God, mature themselves spiritually, and find their place in God's Kingdom is a top priority. Discipleship is a process whereby the result will be each joint giving to the whole in such a way that this diversity in unity brings about corporate maturity. God's Word tells us that,

> Discipleship is a process whereby the result will be each joint giving to the whole in such a way that this diversity in unity brings about corporate maturity.

For we are His workmanship, created in Christ Jesus for good works, which God prepared beforehand, that we should walk in them.[145] Part of every local church's plan for discipleship and growth needs to include a plan for the self-discovery of these truths. The church scores as each person find their place in God's endeavor.

God is calling in this hour to all who will listen. He calls all to find this place and occupy it to His glory. God has unique assignments for each and has provided the resources to fulfill them. He has designed and gifted each person uniquely. When each person finds this place in God and contributes time, talents and assets to this end, God's church grows and moves the Kingdom forward. The Christian walk was never to be walked in solitude independent of others. Finding and occupying this place is the duty of every follower.

8.6 PACE

I grew up in Indiana. Indiana was known for the "Granddaddy" of automobile racing, The Indianapolis 500. As a child, my dad would take my two brothers and me to watch the time trials. These were run just days before the actual race. During the time trials, each driver would have to qualify for the big race by demonstrating how fast they could go. Only one car could be on the track at a time. This scene was very different from the race day event. On race day, the entire field of qualifying cars was lined up behind a pace car. This car was tasked with the assignment of pacing the cars before the start of the race and during caution flags. All the cars had to stay behind the pace car. Once the pace car was off the track, the race was on. In the event of an accident, the pace car would be brought back out onto the track to realign the cars.

Unfortunately, many followers do not follow the spiritual pace car called the Holy Spirit. The pace of ministry is hard to determine, but the results of overextending oneself beyond God's grace has devastating consequences. As a Senior Pastor, it has been difficult over the years to regulate ministry pace. The timing of when to expand the ministry had to be closely monitored. I am sure many leaders burn out and leave the ministry altogether. The job of a spiritual leader can be demanding but being called into the service of Christ is the greatest privilege.

My position, as Senior Pastor and leader of RockFish Church, has been one of the greatest times of my life. The ability to face the challenges of each day comes from God Himself. His grace has allowed me to, not only continue in ministry but find joy each day I serve Him and His people. I have to be keenly aware of the stress and busyness of the duties, and I have to pace myself, not only because of the amount of work involved but because it is addicting to be used by God. We must remember, we didn't die on a cross for anyone and our strength comes from Jesus. Considering this reality, I am not that important. I do get to make positive things happen every day, but it's all about giving back to Jesus what He has already won.

It is important to have people around you who can help you see the big picture and keep you from overextending yourself. I do believe in the realization that the Body needs every part and even the seemingly less prominent pieces are just as critical as any leadership position. We all get to do this! Together! The price has been paid, our success is sure, and the power is available to make it happen. Each person has a job given to them by God, and each is to walk in them successfully. The important thing is to keep an eye on how overly important we perceive ourselves to be. Understanding Jesus and His power, love, and acceptance for His people, we should never try to pick up the heavy end of the load. Jesus does all the heavy lifting. When we get properly yoked up with Him, He will teach us not to run ahead of Him or lag. If our eyes stay fixed upon Him, the pace will become a non-issue.

8.7 PRIORITIES

> Setting aside space to connect with God and get His direction and infilling is necessary to these drastic life changes.

The best way to check the correct priority of activities begins with a look at the individual's ability to incorporate the Spiritual Life Design Protocols (SLDP). These may look different from another disciple's way of connection to God; however, asking God how to incorporate them into day to day life will help guide the process. Bible reading, repenting retreating, worshiping, meditating, memorizing, connective praying, fasting, sabbath keeping, giving, and contemplating are the key ingredients to priority setting. Setting aside both thought and time are needed to be devoted to the discovery of how God calls each into these disciplines. Setting aside space to connect with God and get His direction and infilling is necessary to make these drastic life changes.

While checking the time allotted for the SLDP, it is necessary to take a good look at the Physical Life Design Protocols (PLDP). Time must be allotted for the priorities of eating, sleeping, resting, distressing, exercising, drinking good water, relating, loving, thinking, and avoiding toxins in one's personal life. Attention to both areas (PLDP and SLDP), when developing a proper set of margins, will help as a guide to align with God's design. Healthy growth stems from placing the proper weight upon each of these areas. The interplay of each protocol enhances the whole through Holistic Energetic Coherence (HEC) synchronization. When life is holistically integrated, the power for living is enhanced. God has called us to live an abundant life, not a script of rules. Our lives are not segmented but are to be lived out to the fullest. The Bible states that we are to "pray without ceasing." Praying nonstop can only be a reality if the person is integrated body, soul, and spirit with these energies reciprocally functioning properly.

When the pressure of "shoulds" becomes guilt and condemnation, the forces of shame are afoot. Shame ties the believer to self-dependence and trying to earn favor and acceptance. When people "should on themselves," their ability to move forward becomes hampered, and nothing is accomplished. The Bible makes a clear distinction between condemnation and conviction. Condemnation cripples the follower and leaves him/her frozen in defeat. Conviction comes from the Holy Spirit and empowers the disciple toward life change. Establishing good priorities is the guiding force that moves the follower toward the direction of God's goal--the Gospel. Salvation is all of grace and only through the redemption story is life change realized. Making the name of Jesus spectacular is the glorifying effect of pointing to Him. Apart from the priority of the teachings of Christ and the power derived from the Gospel, the church cannot have any hope for healthy growth. Our purpose is to bring glory to the King of Kings.

Years ago, I did a study on all the "shoulds" of the Christian life. I looked at what the Bible taught and what teachers were saying the walk with Jesus should look like (I made an Excel spreadsheet). The things on the list were things like a study time with God, praying with family, attending church services, evangelistic activities, keeping the Sabbath, and small group participation. I looked at sleep time, work schedule, and vacations. I did not think that I exaggerated any of the "shoulds" (In fact, I think I was conservative in all my time allotments). The results confirmed what I believed to be true; Christians are about 75 days short a year from doing all the activities placed upon them. A lack of days to complete all activities means that the Christian's life is supernatural and easily overextended. It is important to keep marginal management as a top priority. This specific PLDP assists in almost every arena of life. Being overextended is being unavailable for God's mission.

It takes a tremendous amount of grace-filled power to follow Jesus. We cannot hide behind the reality that the walk is supernatural. God will call all of us into account for what we did with what we had been given. He has graced us with all the power needed for life and godliness. Our duty then becomes one of priorities and trust. We cannot afford to become apathetic, because we do not have enough time to complete what is given, but to steward the time well and maintain good priorities in our lives. And, sometimes to say, "no." When managing margin in life, it is important to remember that, for the Christian, this life lived is an exchanged life. Without the building up of reserves in every area of existence, it is unlikely that the true purpose and calling of life will be discovered. Without resiliency, produced by managing margin, life burns out and finishing well never materializes.

The disciple-makers, especially governmental church leadership, should help the individual church member discover the power of these healthy lifestyle efforts. Developing a strategy that allows for, and takes into consideration these important life needs, will help the Body of Christ become all she is intended to become. More intentionality in this approach is needed in every church. Filling the church calendar with activity is easy. Just remember, that every event pulls on the priorities and energies of individual lives. The church strategy needs to include down-times. The church culture should include the element of freedom that allows members to "not be there." When pressure, whether stated directly or implied, is placed upon people to be there every time the church doors are open, an unhealthy expectation is created that will lead to congregational burnout. Recognizing overcommitment becomes critical as the church grows. When the church grows numerically, services and events are added. People need to feel released to "not be there." This church growth transition is difficult, but it is very necessary for the church to grow. The leadership must make this a priority as the church grows. This is accomplished through communication and modeling.

I have discovered at RockFish Church that as she grew, and more activities were added, I had less and less idea of what was happening on any given day. I had to learn to be ok with this. Currently, RockFish has six full live worship services every week at the same location. There are also activities every day of the week (some of them I have never attended). I had to be secure with letting others lead the services. It was strange at first, but for me to maintain my and the church's spiritual and physical health, I had to learn to let go. If the leader must have his hands in everything, I can assure you that the flock will not grow in a healthy way. Letting others discover their gifts and callings has been one of the greatest joys of being a pastor. The fruit of multiplying myself through others in ministry has been an important factor in RockFish's history. I believe as time goes on, the fruit of this permission-granting culture will produce a multitude of life-transforming stories.

8.8 PRESENCE

The Church can never become or stay in a state of human invention. Drawing crowds to a location for the applause of men will not bring about the righteousness of God. If the value of church growth is getting more people to attend meetings alone, the goal has become the problem. Bringing more and more people to a building without realizing that it is

God who calls people to Himself will produce the mentality of trying to get God to bless our good ideas. The Church is His invention. He called us to come out and come away from the ways of the world. Coming out of the world includes using worldly thinking to increase church attendance.

The church's ability to successfully foster God's presence will determine healthy corporate growth. We must guard, with the utmost diligence, an environment conducive to God's Holy Spirit. We cannot afford to miss this. The Holy Spirit's presence is the only generating force for life change. If lives are not changing in our services, there is no need to meet. Redemption of body, soul, and spirit can only happen by the hand of God. He is the Way, the Truth, and the Life. Apart from Him, we can do nothing. Anything good that takes place in our churches only comes from Him. Jesus paid the heavy price to bring the church into existence, and we cannot have a church without Him. He invented the Church, created Her, sustains Her, and will bring Her to Her destiny. We beat up the enemy because of the blood of the Lamb, the word of our testimony, and not loving our lives—even to the point of death. We don't have any claim to the purchasing of humanity; Jesus paid it all. We can proclaim Him and turn away from self. Reducing self is our duty.

> The church's ability to successfully foster God's presence will determine healthy corporate growth.

An individual or congregation that does not take the reality of God's abiding presence seriously will not experience the joy of operating in the center of God's will. Hidden sin, minimization of the importance of His abiding grace, or compromise will short-circuit spiritual growth. It is important for all of the leaders to be accountable to the leadership as a group. The critical nature of the theocracy in the local church allows for the leadership body to act as judges that apply God's Word to individuals for accountability. Leaders are accountable to the teachings of Jesus as applied by the leadership board. The follower must abide in Him. The follower that is living in the disintegration of the soul, not realizing the importance of God's presence, will experience no real growth and waste valuable time. The importance of living for Him, in front of Him, keeps the disciple moving spiritually in the right direction.

Cultivating this reality will help keep every aspect of life thriving. Living out life to glorify Jesus brings power to our purpose. Finding one's meaning in temporary things that ultimately fail is a cheap substitute for the design and plan of God. So much of life becomes sideways energy and detracts from fulfilling the intention of God and the enjoyment of His presence. Having Holy Spirit operation in the daily events of life carries with it the great personal benefit of joy and inner peace.

We can, however, frustrate—and even grieve—the Holy Spirit, making individual and corporate spiritual growth impossible. It is imperative for church leadership to cultivate and protect a culture that is Holy Spirit friendly. A person can have all the great blessings of this world, but without God's abiding presence, one can miss the true meaning of life. Having material blessings but grieving the Spirit will disintegrate in the long-run, and it hampers the work of Christ. The Church can develop great innovative strategies and execute practical ministry with good intentions, but if God is grieved, the eternal outcome will not be realized. Grieving the Holy Spirit happens whenever there are sins and compromise. I am not talking about our lack of following God perfectly. What I am talking about is secret sin or hypocrisy.

The Bible teaches us, *So then, my beloved, just as you have always obeyed, not as in my presence only, but now much more in my absence, work out your salvation with fear and trembling; for it is God who is at work in you, both to will and to work for His good pleasure.*[146] The fact that God is at work while we are in process should posture us in fearful reverence. This verse explains that God not only helps us to perform godly tasks but even works deep within us to help motivate us. The realization that the Creator Himself works within each follower and in the church is overwhelming.

We live in a great time of innovation and the ability to have the church services enhanced; but, if innovation becomes the end, His presence will be replaced with man's ideas and the catering of activities to please the Western mindset. God's ways are higher than ours. His attendance must be the driving priority of all activities. I love to see people attend church and leave transformed. I live to see people being made into the image of Christ, to see the true worshipping of His people, and lives surrendering to the Gospel. His Bride will be beautiful when she matures into the Lady He paid so much for Her to become. When She demonstrates Her love for Her Savior and love for each other, there is great rejoicing in heaven. Watching Her grow and mature into His lady is the joy of being a pastor. Helping Her step into Her designed place is every believer's responsibility.

9

CONCLUSION

Transforming G.R.O.W.T.H. implementation is an emphasis on a holistic approach toward the integration of the whole person as they spiritually mature. The command to love the Lord with everything is more than a set of unrelated rules. It is the universal life operational construct designed by God. This command fuels the cosmos. The outward-focused nature of loving God and others finds its core within the pre-fallen state of this planet. God is love, and love is outward focused. Overcoming the broken nature of humanity can only be achieved through the Gospel of Jesus Christ and restoring the divine order of love.

The goal of healthy spiritual growth is not to build big churches but the facilitating of the greatness of the Church that will magnify the Savior of the world. Healthy spiritual growth carries with it the benefit of being used by God throughout the believer's lifetime. Churches and individuals that cooperate with God's design will experience vitality, peace, and power for living that outlasts themselves and grows the Church into the next generation.

In this challenging time, it is imperative that the Church take Her position and fulfill Her destiny. She must posture Herself with the high value of proclaiming the Gospel throughout the Earth that will allow the Good News to reach every creature. Blocks to Her progress must be removed, and each person in the Kingdom must evaluate his/her spiritual health. Distractions are many and sideways energy must be overcome. A singular focused Church will accomplish Her directive. Understanding the culture surrounding each church, and applying God's message to that culture, is the duty of the governmental leadership of the body. Affirming certain cultural needs without compromising the teachings of Jesus is the proper position. Removal of distortionary blocks and man-made traditions, while maintaining a non-compromising stance of truth, becomes the Church's modality for proper growth. This stance of culturally-relevant Holy Spirit-sensitive churches is what is needed across the Western world.

Prioritizing the Great Commandment, along with the Great Commission, helps direct all the activities of a church that facilitates life-transformation. Creating churches that keep these main objectives as the driving forces of Kingdom movements is the job of all leaders. These servant leaders are watchkeepers of this holy calling and vision given to the Church by God. The church culture that effectively and efficiently keeps the Kingdom priority forefront will allow for an environment of healthy spiritual growth. Conversely, compromising the main mandates from God of loving Him, loving people, teaching Biblical standards, baptizing, evangelizing, and making disciples, will only foster spiritual sickness and weakness.

A multitude of factors guides the endeavor of discipling individuals and congregations into healthy spiritual growth. Keeping the Gospel God in view is the foundation of all spiritual growth and becomes the keystone of spiritual maturity. Connection to Him as the true-life force, maintaining the concept that it is all about proper relationship with Him and others, guides the entire process. Being influenced by the saving work of Jesus Christ and influencing others gives the needed positive tension that helps the edification process. Bringing all areas of human experience into worshiping God totally: body, soul, and spirit, allows for the fulfillment of the call. It is important to realize that all parts of life need redeeming. The body is the temple of the Holy Spirit. Stewarding this great resource physically, emotionally, mentally, and spiritually is critical. This philosophy, guided by the governmental leadership of the church, will ensure that the church's trajectory will keep moving toward the vision God intended.

Our response to God is first, repentance. Turning from our natural ways and toward God's laws heals the fractured soul and allows for complete healing in all areas of life. Response repentance is a life typified by a focus upon the guidance of the Holy Spirit. Holy Spirit guidance gives the needed power to grow toward the wholeness God intends. The spiritual discipline of repentance in response to God requires asking God for necessary wisdom. As we traverse this life, God assures us the promise of receiving this wisdom.

A church that stays Gospel-focused and motivated moves into a place of spiritual blessing. Having a church culture that understands how to connect the broken needs of the world around it, with the life-giving force of the love of God, will result in a powerful place of transformative redemption. A church that can incarnate the work of Christ into every-day life-connections will never see a lack of hungry seekers wanting this reality. The Church has been given the stewardship of life transformation through the power of the Gospel of Jesus Christ. The opportunities for applying the truth of God's Word is without end. The healthy church is a church with healthy followers of Jesus that understand the eternal ramification of obeying the assignment of God to "go."

The proper Physical Life Dynamic Protocols (PLDP) keep the physical life issues from interfering with God's purpose for the life of individuals as well as churches. Being available and maintaining availability to be used by God is the goal of understanding the Life Design Protocols (LDP). This total surrender to the PLDP and Spiritual Life Dynamic Protocols (SLDP) is a life-long process. As the disciple seeks to become more and more like the Master, his/her life will become conformed into His likeness. Most difficulties that have surfaced in my years as a follower and a Christian counselor resulted from holding back part of the total being. Withholding parts of a person's life may be the consequence of past traumas, character flaws, or open sin. The major blocks to living a lifestyle of worship stem from the inability to process the grace given by God. He has given us everything to live this life and do it in a godly manner. The selfishness of withholding anything from God blocks the very grace needed to grow in Him.

The Omega Optic of a healthy church is a vision that sees the top priority of loving God and loving people. The message of the Gospel is one of love connection made vertically as well as horizontally. Acceptance of people and loving them enough to tell them the truth is the hallmark of a healthy growing church. This connection facilitates the move of the Holy Spirit as He loves people through the Church. Where the Church is healthy, the fruit of the Spirit is evident and celebrated. Removal of anything that would grieve the Holy Spirit becomes essential. The application of the cross of Jesus Christ includes the redemption of all areas of mankind. Allowing unconfessed sin to root itself in the Body of Christ will result in spiritual sickness. God loves the sinner but has remedied the problem at a great cost. The magnitude of the effects of unconfessed sin is not to be taken lightly or without great care by His followers.

As the whole person is connected to God and His principles, worship is metabolized, and the believers experience God's wonders. The spirit, soul, and body of a disciple that has been surrendered at the feet of Jesus experience undeniable power. The spirit of man, when undergoing salvation, results in a power that is given to bring life transformation throughout the entire essence of the person. True healthy spiritual growth cannot be achieved while having a fractured soul. The full redemptive work of Christ is best displayed through a sanctified body, soul, and spirit. True worship is total worship realized through spirit and truth. The human body is the temple of the Holy Spirit that is made to experience abundant life in Jesus. As abundant life is expressed, the fullness of joy is experienced. The (SLDP) bring the result of the connection to this grace of God as is supplied through the power of the Holy Spirit. Joy, full of glory, is the lifestyle result of worship. Righteousness, peace, and joy are the products of the complete Kingdom operation as the believer surrenders his/her total life to Jesus.

The Church, likewise, must become a collective culture of denying self and moving in the grace God offers. The stumbling blocks to this grace formulate from multiple combinations of fear, unbelief, unconfessed sin, unforgiveness, unregeneration, and hypocrisy. Corporate worship will suffer if the culture of the Body of Christ allows these spiritual blocks. The governmental leadership of the church must keep a close eye on leanings toward any of these grace inhibitors. Jesus paid a high price for His Bride to become a kingdom of sold-out worshipers. The very virtues displayed in Christ should be the goal of His followers. The Church has been given the power, forgiveness, and promises through the completed work of Christ. It should be the goal of every believer and church to surrender to Him and experience true life-transforming worship.

God has given the prescription for a healthy personal, family, and church structure. As the bones hold up the body, the structure holds up His Body. The theocratic tapestry seen throughout the Scripture exhibits the proper design for this structure. Lives built squarely upon the governance of God's Word are critical for proper spiritual development and the capacity to glorify God. From the Old Testament to the governmental structure of the early New Testament church, the importance of the theocratic structure and the result of poor structures have been seen. Allowing the Holy Spirit to apply the Scripture to all areas of life is the hallmark of a good fundamental structure. When the theocratic application is not followed, the results become foundational cracks in lives, families, and churches. But, when God's plan for governance is followed, the outcome is the glorification of the Father.

The goal of godly leadership is to create a healthy spiritual culture. The culture of a growing, life-giving church gains its power from reliance upon Jesus and His Life-giving Spirit. The Holy Spirit is the source of power, direction, and grace. As each player in God's grand story takes their place in the Body, spiritual growth will become apparent. Unity, power, purpose, priority, and God's presence become the driving forces that move the Kingdom of God forward. As the individual members of the Body position themselves properly and give to the group their unique gifting and resources, the growth of the church advances in a healthy, dynamic way.

The power of the individual, and of the Church, is derived from the Gospel. Any substitute for this power will eventually end in spiritual sickness. The communication of this truth carries the very power that was used to create and sustain the universe. The belief that it is possible to outgrow the Gospel demonstrates a lack in understanding the very nature of God's purpose in the Earth and the power of life-transformation that only happens through the Gospel. The Gospel is the portal of going deep into God. The Gospel requires an ever-increasing, decrease of the self life of the disciple. Many would be satisfied with more and more knowledge of spiritual matters. However, the deepest things of God are found in the Grand Story of God's redeeming love that was accomplished through His gift of reconciliation; His Son, Jesus Christ.

Working toward and anticipating healthy spiritual growth is very much like flying a plane. Perfect textbook conditions in which to land the bird occurs rarely. The application of this topic will never involve perfect circumstances. A spiritual journey is just that, a journey. Lives are never lived in flawless conditions, and the principles of spiritual growth work out differently depending upon the context. God has given us His design that, if followed, will produce healthy growth. The need for healthy spiritual growth then becomes dependent upon our ability to draw near to God. Getting close to Jesus and hearing His heart's cry will transform our eyes to see the way He sees. Letting go of the agendas of this life and stopping long enough to have the Holy Spirit lead us into this adventure brings with it the thrill of working alongside God, Himself.

As I write the conclusion to this book, the effects of hurricane Florence are still being felt in my home in North Carolina. Summer was intruded upon by this massive storm that took out our power, septic, gas stations, and even closed Walmart. The hurricane threw trees down in my yard with a terrifying vengeance, slicing through power lines, and blocking the driveway. The church was sealed up, and all six services were canceled. Life was certainly disrupted on many levels. Weeks after the storm, the church congregation still labors to help everyone dig out of this intruding storm that disrupted life. Florence remains the topic of everyone's conversation. Flood waters are just now receding. People lost houses, jobs, comforts, and some even lost their lives.

Life is living with the ever-present possibility of such storms. Life is messy, and the expectation of life-uninterrupted is false. Building your house upon the foundation of Jesus will prove to be a structure that will survive the many storms of life. The teachings of Jesus exclaim that rain is coming, floods will happen, and wind will blow. The life built according to His design will stand. A life built on any other foundation will fall, and its fall will be great.[87] Building a life according to Transforming G.R.O.W.T.H. will allow for the resiliency and the perseverance needed to take this Kingdom Gospel to the ends of the Earth. Life carries with it the ravages of sin that has left the human condition fragmented and latent with emotional pain. This condition hinders many from experiencing the necessary soul environment for proper growth. Churches, as well, experience these disturbances. Godly influencers can help bring the needed healing and direction. As embedded lies are replaced with the truth of God through repentance, freedom from the past becomes a reality. Repentance married with faith is the two-legged process of the Christian walk. Faith in the substitutionary work of Christ, as a way of life, increases spiritual awareness and growth. Turning from the old self-life to the life God intended will result in the Gospel power needed for life change.

Our God-given purpose is to proclaim the Good News of God's clemency, calling, and compassion. The Church is not needed for the salvation of individuals, but it is needed to announce the Great News to a crippled, dying world. The power of the Church is often underestimated. She is the principal agent of the Earth to herald the salvation story and demonstrate God's power through weak vessels. The manifold expression of God's grace spreads across a wide range of individual life-stories that brings magnification to the finished work of Jesus Christ. The expression of this purpose may appear unique in the individual application across different churches, but the goal is always the same. The goal of all churches is the redemption of humanity and their culture.

The leader must always touch the Bride of Jesus with clean hands and a clean heart. It is vital that leaders keep themselves healthy in all aspects of life. Self-check and accountability become necessary to ensure that the grace of God is being utilized in all life protocols. The greatest thing the leader can do is fall more and more in love with Jesus. Many forces are pulling the follower in various directions. Fighting the good fight is a fight for our attention and affection. Positioning the soul to love God in an integrated way allows for spiritual health which translates into effective ministry. Our lives were purchased to be spent advancing the Kingdom.

Watching RockFish grow and discover Her destiny is akin to watching my children grow and develop. Like an overprotective parent, my day is filled with watchful care and a desire to do my part to see Her become all She was intended to become. The main force of seeing Her Master's Name made spectacular and known allows me the strength to daily face the challenges of laying my life down and leading God's people forward. I am keenly aware of His heart for His people as I help move people toward maturity and away from brokenness, hurt, and bondage. My work for the Gospel is fueled by my own need for this Great Savior. As I touch His Bride, I do so with holy fear and the realization that Jesus died for these people.

I have discovered, as I watched RockFish Church grow from eleven families into a healthy community of followers, that Jesus desires His Bride to mature and become all He paid for Her to become. The eagerness of God to see His people grow in a healthy manner far exceeds anyone else's motivation. He truly loves His Church beyond measure. Finding the joy of the Father as lives are transformed has become the driving force of this pastor.

APPENDIX A1 –
COUNSELING INTAKE FORM WITH LDP

www.RockFishChurch.com

RockFish Church

Net-Working for Jesus   Dan Stanley, Senior Pastor

RockFish Church holds to the ideal that a person's confidentially shared information should be held in the highest trust. During counseling information may be shared for the purpose of relational reconciliation. This information should only be used to grow deeper in relationship to God and each other. In regards to any and all information shared during counseling sessions, phone calls or any other scenario where a pastor's counsel is sought and obtained, the counseling pastor of a RockFish Church member is not required to release this information, in written or verbal form, to any third party based on confidentiality rights between a minister and a church member as stated in North Carolina General Statute Sec. 8-53.2*, 8-53.6 and 8-56. It should be understood that a judge can order that such information be made public. If this order is given by a judge, this information will only be given under protest of the violation of the confessional right between a minister and the parishioner. The only exception to this rule is the determination of the minister that a person or persons may be in physical danger or the suspect of possible child abuse.

Signature   Date

_____   _____

NC General Statue 8-53.2. Communications between clergymen and communicants.
No priest, rabbi, accredited Christian Science practitioner, or a clergyman or ordained minister of an established church shall be competent to testify in any action, suit or proceeding concerning any information which was communicated to him and entrusted to him in his professional capacity, and necessary to enable him to discharge the functions of his office according to the usual course of his practice or discipline, wherein such person so communicating such information about himself or another is seeking spiritual counsel and advice relative to and growing out of the information so imparted, provided, however, that this section shall not apply where communicant in open court waives the privilege conferred. (1959, c. 646; 1963, c. 200; 1967, c. 794.)

See also § 8-53.8. Counselor privilege, § 8-53.5. Communications between licensed marital and family therapist and client(s)., § 8-53.6. No disclosure in alimony and divorce actions.

9949 Fayetteville Road
Raeford, NC 28376

Dr. Dan Stanley-Pastor
(910)875-5680

Counseling Intake Information
(Confidential)

(print clearly)

Date:_____   Name:_____

Address:_____

Phone (home):_____ Phone (w or c):_____

Male____ Female____ Race____ Age____ Date of birth:_____

Place of Birth:_____ Referred by:_____

What is the main reason for this counseling appt?_____

Family Doctor:_____

Living Arrangement: Own___ Rent___ Other_____ How long at this address?_____

Number of addresses in last 10 years:_____ Financial problems? No ___ Yes ___

	Counselee	Spouse
Employer:	_____	_____
Job Title:	_____	_____
Years at:	_____	_____

Are you adopted?_____ When?_____ At what age?_____

Any childhood sickness or injuries (give age and details)

_____

_____

Describe your earliest Memory:_____

_____

_____

Current medications:_____

Hereditary diseases?_____

List physical impairments:_____

Have you ever had venereal disease?_____

History of Mental Illness?_____ Did it result in hospitalization?_____

Ever attempted suicide?_____

Height:_____ Weight:_____ Any change in weight?_____

Date of last physical:_____

Problems with: Compulsive eating?___ Nervous eating?___ Inability to eat?___

What is your greatest fear?_____

Have you ever lost someone close to you through death? Yes/No
If Yes: What was your relationship?_____
Also, please give details: _____
_____

I feel closest to_____ I feel least close to _____
The person who has had the greatest influence in my life is_____
Why?_____
Were you able to confide in your parents? Yes/No
Home was _____(happy, etc.)
In what ways were you punished?_____
_____

Were your parents separated or divorced? _____Which parent raised you?___
Did your parents remarry_____

_____

Mark an "X" in the box that best describes your feelings for your father and an "O" for
your mother.

	1	2	3	4	5	
Strong						Weak
Warm						Cold
Close						Distant
Happy						Sad
Good						Bad
Interested						Uninterested
Smart						Stupid
Loving						Hateful
Masculine						Feminine
industrious						Lazy
Generous						Stingy
Healthy						Sick
Accepting						Critical
Strict						Lax
Rich						Poor

My parents were _____ parents.
I was closest to my _____. My parents punished me (in relationship to your brothers or sisters) more or less than _____
Education level _____ How many grammar schools? _____
Ever take special classes? _____ Explain _____
Did you ever have difficulties in school? _____
Athletics: Active _____ Average _____ Less than average _____
Grade point average: _____ Popularity: _____
Amount of dating in high school: _____

Marital History
Marital status ____ Date of marriage: _____ Spouse's Name_____
How long did you know your spouse before marriage? _____ Did you engage in pre-marital sex? _____ Name and Age of Children:_____
_____
Were you pregnant at the time of marriage? Yes/No
Is your sex life with your spouse satisfactory? _____ If no, explain:_____
_____
Have you been married before? _____ How long?_____ Have there been any threats of violence from your spouse? YES/NO Has there been actual violence?_____
How are conflicts handled within your marriage? _____
How is love and caring displayed in your marriage?_____
_____
Are you satisfied with your marriage? _____ Why?_____
_____
How could your marriage be improved? _____
_____

General Sexual History
When and how did you learn about sex? _____
_____
Are you or have you been sexually active outside of marriage? _____
Have you ever had a negative sexual experience?_____

Physical Life Activities
On average, how many hours of sleep do you get each night? _____
What type of water do you drink? (Pick 1) Well ____ Municipal _____ or Bottle _____
Would you say your stress level is; Low ____ Average _____ High _____ Very high ____
What type of diet do you have?
        Standard American Diet ____ Vegan _____ Protein _____ Other _____
        describe _____
Describe your level of physical activity _____
What type of neighborhood do you live? Country _____ Urban _____ City _____

Spiritual Life Activities
Do you spend time each week ... In Prayer? _____ Bible Reading? _____ Fasting? ____
Meditating? _____ Fellowshipping?_____ Attending Church? _____
In a Small Group? _____
Do you take one day a week and give it to God? _____

APPENDIX A2 –

DR. STANLEY BEFORE THE UNITED NATIONS SPEAKING ON BEHALF OF THE SAHRAWI PEOPLE'S RIGHT FOR SELF-DETERMINATION. (72LBS HEAVIER)

APPENDIX A3 –
KEY ACRONYMS AND TERMS

- **LDP** – Life Design Protocols
- **PLDP** – Physical Life Design Protocols
- **SLDP** – Spiritual Life Design Protocols
- **RCIIH** – Reciprocal Cybernetic Inductional Interaction Hypothesis is the hypothesis of the separate but parallel waves of influence between systems of the body, soul, and spirit without physical contact.
- **PEPBIF** – Pneuma-energeticpsychobio interaction factor healing is the counseling descriptor used in the emotional healing of locked up incorrect emotional responses due to embedded lies inserted during the developmental stages of childhood growth. Schemas with locked up memory blocks caused by false interpretations of one's safety, purpose, value or future expectations and future image are changed using the Holy Spirit's guidance to exchange the believed lie with the truth. These imprintings are usually developed between the ages of pre-birth and 14 years. Inserting of the proper interpretations into the faulty memory block frees the person. The principle of pneuma-energeticpsychobio Interaction factor (PEPBIF) is the realignment of the body, soul and spirit hierarchy whereas the spirit of the person is empowered by the Holy Spirit to lead them in all aspects of life. Proper PEPBIF allows for deep healing to take place and is the proper functioning of the follower's daily LDP. Minding the things of the spirit increases truth in the inner man. ("you will know the truth, and the truth will set you free").
- **HEC** - Holistic energetic coherence is the optimum energy output from all of the systems related to RCIIH. When HEC's are in sync complete worship of God is in spirit and truth.

- **IPNB** stands for Interpersonal Neurobiology (first developed by Dan Siegel and Allan Schore) is the primary theory and practical working model which describes human development and function as being a product of the relationship between body, mind, and relationships. It includes but is not limited to the effects of social-genomics (effects of relationships on genetics).

- **Biophotonic**: The biophotonic nature of the energetic capabilities of the heart to emit lazar-like emissions to imprint DNA causing methylation and histone modification.
- **Cerebral cortex** is the outer layer of the cerebrum composed of folded gray matter and playing an important role in consciousness.
- **Cognitive Dissonance** – the inconsistency of thoughts, values or beliefs within one's self
- **Emotional Intelligence** entails five different skill sets; 1) self-awareness, 2) self-regulation, 3) social skills, 4) empathy, and 5) motivation. It may be thought of as the measure of the awareness of one's emotions and the ability to grasp and navigate interpersonal relationships.
- **Epigenetics** is the set of alteration of genetic material that modifies gene expression. Genetic DNA tags are switched on or off but don't alter the genes themselves. It also influences histone performance.
- **Eudaimonics**, pronounced "you-demonics" is concerned with self-actualization and wellbeing.
- **Glymphatic system** is the functional waste removal pathway of the brain. (more on this protocol result of the PLDP; Restorative Sleep in chapter five.)
- **Hedonics** is the philosophy of life that celebrates pleasure over discomfort and pain.
- **Hermeneutics** is the science or methodology of Biblical interpretation.

- **Histones** are the chief primary proteins of chromatin, which DNA winds around acting as spools. They control gene regulation.
- **Interactive Biology** looks at interactions of the environment, whole-organism biology including genetic, cellular, and morphological processes.
- **Limbic brain** is involved in motivation, emotion, learning, and memory. The limbic system is where the subcortical structures meet the cerebral cortex.
- **Locus of control** is the notion or perception that the individual is the source of control of differing situations. The proposition here is that believers have limits to their control and must depend upon God as the ultimate external locus of control.
- **Marginal Management** – Managing the space between resources and life requirements
- **Methylation** can change the "on and off" switching tags that changes the DNA expressional activity without changing the sequence.
- **Molecules of Emotions** – referenced in the book by that title describing the link between consciousness, mind, and body
- **Munificence** used here as a spiritual discipline of God-like generosity
- **Negentropic** is life's ability to reduce entropy (and corresponding increase in order). Life has the ability to take food (dead material) for instance and apply forces to it to produce energy towards order.
- **Neurobiology** is the biology of the nervous system.
- **Neuroception** is the ability of the neural circuitry (affecting the autonomic nervous system) to evaluate risk in the environment without awareness or cognition. See the book The Polyvagal Theory by Dr. Steven Porges, (New York, New York, W.W. Norton & Company; 2017).
- **Neurogenesis** is the birthing of new neurons through neuroplasticity of the brain. This allows for a new way of thinking

transformatively which can even produce new genetic expressions physiologically.

- **Nihilism** is the belief that life is random and is meaningless.
- **Nutrigenomics** is the scientific study of the interaction of nutrition and genes, especially with regard to the prevention or treatment of disease.
- **Nutrigenomics** – The study of the interaction of nutrition and genetics.
- **Parasympathetic Nervous System** responds to support homeostasis, health, growth, and restoration. It also has the capacity to shut down life functions.
- **Ponderostatic** is the brain's functional system purposed for weight regulation.
- **Psychogenic** needs explain the need for power, affiliation, and achievement and its impact on influencing others.
- **Psychon** – hypothetical particle of conscience
- **Relational Biology** is a branch of mathematical biophysics relating to the connectedness and bio-topological nature of complex systems.
- **Restorative Sleep** – Sleep needed to cleanse the brain of toxins and waste byproducts fully
- **Sabbath** is the spiritual discipline of restorative weekly connection to God by His Spirit and the reality that Christ has finished the work of redemption and given His followers the power of life change that works every day.
- **Self-reductionism** is used here in the context of willfully reducing self in light of promoting spiritual growth (spiritual reduction of self which allows healthy growth in the inner man). **Sinus arrhythmia** – The normal increase in heart rate that occurs during inspiration (when breathing in quickly).
- **Social engagement system** connects the heart with the muscles of the face and head. There is a direct correlation between the two through the somatomotor component pathways of the vagus system.

- **Sociogenomics** looks at how social factors affect the genome and its expression.
- **Somatotopic** is relating to or mediating the relation between particular body parts and corresponding motor areas of the brain.
- **Sympathetic Nervous System** in response to danger reacts to increase blood flow throughout the body to support fight/flight behaviors.
- **Takotsubo cardiomyopathy** – cardiogenic shock due to loss or extreme emotional situation which can lead to death if not treated right away.
- **Telomeres** are compound structures at the end of the chromosome. They deteriorate over time and can determine biological age.
- **Telomere Resiliency** is the slowing of the rate of the biological aging process. Telomeres protect the ends of the DNA. They are protective sheaths of proteins that are used up during cell division.
- **Thermoregulatory** is the brain's functional system purposed for heat regulation of the body.
- **Visceral** – Referring to the internal organs of the body. Visceral is felt "deep down." It is the "gut feeling." Visceral reactions proceed from instinct rather than intellect.

BIBLIOGRAPHY

1. George Barna, "AMERICAN CULTURE REVIEW": *Groundbreaking ACFI Survey Reveals How Many Adults Have a Biblical Worldview,* https://www.culturefaith.com/groundbreaking-survey-by-acfi-reveals-how-many-american-adults-have-a-biblical-worldview/, (accessed March 9, 2017).
2. Julia Duin, *Quitting Church: Why the Faithful Are Fleeing and What to Do About It.* (Grand Rapids, Michigan: Baker House, 2008), 12
3. Ephesians 2:6
4. L. Frank Baum, *The Wizard of Oz.* (Strand, London: Penguin Group, Puffin Books, 1982), 3
5. L. Frank Baum, The Wizard of Oz. (Strand, London: Penguin Group, Puffin Books, 1982)
6. Ibid., 46-47
7. Ibid., 53
8. Luke 24:30-35
9. Romans 16:20
10. L. Frank Baum, *The Wizard of Oz.* (Strand, London: Penguin Group, Puffin Books, 1982), 86
11. Ibid., 89-90
12. Ephesians 4:12-13
13. Galatians 2:20
14. Dick Staub, *Christian Wisdom of the Jedi Masters*, (San Francisco, California, Jossey-Bass, 2005), 66
15. Matthew 7:13-14
16. Rick Warren, *The Purpose Driven Church*, (Grand Rapids, Michigan: Zondervan, 1995), 102
17. Ibid., 119
18. John 15:13
19. Thom S. Rainer, *The Unchurched Next Door,* (Grand Rapids, Michigan: Zondervan, 2003), 25
20. Ibid., 25
21. Ibid., 225
22. 1 Corinthians 3:11
23. Ephesians 2:17-22
24. Matt Chandler, Josh Patterson, Eric Geiger, *Creature of The Word: The Jesus-centered Church,* (Nashville, Tennessee: B&H, 2012), 5
25. Mark 16:15-16
26. Matthew 28:18-20
27. Matthew 24:14
28. Revelation 18:4
29. Matthew 10:39
30. Matthew 12:37

31. Romans 12:2
32. Curt Thompson, "A Body of Work: Interpersonal Neurobiology and the Progression of Psychotherapy." (Lecture, American Association of Christian Counselors World Conference, Opryland Hotel, Nashville, TN, September 28, 2017).
33. 1 Corinthians 1:18
34. Genesis 16:13
35. Galatians 5:6
36. Dallas Willard, "Spiritual Formation; What it is, and How it is Done," Dallas Willard Articles. http://www.dwillard.org/articles/artview.asp?artID=58 (accessed October 16,2017).
37. Ephesians 6:12
38. Matthew 23:15
39. 1 Corinthians 14:23
40. Matt Chandler, Josh Patterson, Eric Geiger, *Creature of the Word; The Jesus-centered Church*, (Nashville, Tennessee: B&H, 2012), 205, 206. Gailyn Van Rheenen, *Contextualization and Syncretism,* Monthly Missiological Reflection 38:5
41. Rick Warren, *The Purpose Driven Church,* (Grand Rapids, Michigan, 1995), 15, 16
42. Ibid.
43. Luke 10:27, Deut. 6:5, Lev. 19:18
44. Matt Chandler, Josh Patterson, Eric Geiger, *Creature of The Word: The Jesus-centered Church,* (Nashville, Tennessee: B&H, 2012), 17
45. Romans 1:16-32
46. Matt Chandler, Josh Patterson, Eric Geiger, *Creature of The Word: The Jesus-centered Church,* (Nashville, Tennessee: B&H, 2012), 7-8
47. 1 John 4:19
48. 1 Corinthians 13:1-3
49. Galatians 3:13-14
50. Romans 8:23-14
51. Francis Chan, *Forgotten God: Reversing Our Tragic Neglect of The Holy Spirit,* (Colorado Springs, Colorado: David C. Cook, 2009), 109
52. Revelation 13:8
53. Ephesians 2:6
54. Matthew 24:24
55. 1 John 5:1-5
56. Genesis 2:18
57. Genesis 2:23
58. Ecclesiastes 3:11
59. Acts 17:27-29
60. Glenn G. Dudley, M.D., *Journey to the Center of the Brain: Explaining Mind in a Universe of Matter,* (Lexington, KY, 2011) 29
61. Ibid., 51
62. Proverbs 4:23

63. Curt Thompson, M.D., *Anatomy of The Soul: Surprising Connections Between Neuroscience and Spiritual Practices That Can Transform Your Life and Relationships,* (Carrollton, Texas: Tyndale House, 2010) 120

64. Romans 1:18-20

65. Rob Moll, *What Your Body Knows About God: How We Are Designed to Connect, Serve and Thrive,* (Downers Grove, Illinois: InterVarsity Press, 2014), 40. David Eagleman, *Incognito: The Secret Lives of the Brain,* (New York: Pantheon Books, 2001), 83

66. Curt Thompson, M.D., *Anatomy of The Soul: Surprising Connections Between Neuroscience and Spiritual Practices That Can Transform Your Life and Relationships,* (Carrollton, Texas: Tyndale House, 2010) 112

67. Revelation 21:22

68. 1 Corinthians 3:10-17

69. Matthew 28:19-20

70. Richard A. Swenson, M.D., *Margin: Restoring Emotional, Physical, Financial, and Time Reserve To Overloaded Lives,* (Colorado Springs, CO: NavPress, 2004)

71. Steven W. Porges, Ph.D., *The Pocket Guide to The Polyvagal Theory: The Transformative Power of Feeling Safe,* (New York – London: W.W. Norton & Company, 2017), 68

72. Nessa Carey, Ph.D., *The Epigenetics Revolution: How Modern Biology Is Rewriting Our Understanding of Genetics, Disease, and Inheritance,* (New York, New York: Columbia University Press, 2012), 4,239

73. Steven W. Porges, Ph.D., *The Pocket Guide to The Polyvagal Theory: The Transformative Power of Feeling Safe,* (New York – London: W.W. Norton & Company, 2017), 54-55

74. Ibid.,30

75. Elizabeth Blackburn, Ph.D., Elissa Epel, Ph.D., *The Telomere Effect: A Revolutionary Approach to Living Younger, Healthier, Longer,* (New York, New York: Grand Central Publishing, 2017), 7

76. Galatians 4

77. 1 Thessalonians 5:23

78. Matthew 8:19-22; 10:5-42

79. Matthew 7:21-27

80. Leviticus 25:21

81. Ephesians 4

82. Colossians 1:13-17

83. Hebrews 1:1-3

84. James 1:13-15

85. Jeremiah 17:9

86. Romans 7:14-25

87. 2 Timothy 4:3

88. Psalm 133

89. Matt Chandler, Josh Patterson, Eric Geiger, *Creature of The Word: The Jesus-centered Church,* (Nashville, Tennessee: B&H, 2012), 104

90. Rob Moll, *What Your Body Knows About God: How We Are Designed to Connect, Serve and Thrive,* (Downers Grove, Illinois: InterVarsity Press, 2014), 65

91. Steven W. Porges, Ph.D., *The Pocket Guide to The Polyvagal Theory: The Transformative Power of Feeling Safe,* (New York – London: W.W. Norton & Company, 2017), 51

92. 1 Thessalonians 5:23

93. Matthew 6:9-15

94. James 1:12-18

95. James 4:1-10

96. Romans 8

97. Candace B. Pert, *Molecules of Emotion: The Science Between Mind-Body Medicine,* (New York, New York, Simon and Schuster, 1999)

98. Hebrews 12:5 & Proverbs 14:30

99. Hebrews 4:12

100. John 21

101. Curt Thompson, M.D., *The Soul of Shame: Retelling the Stories We Believe About Ourselves,* (Downers Grove, Illinois: InterVarsity Press, 2015) 62

102. Proverbs 6:6-9

103. Proverbs 20:4-5

104. 1 Chronicles 12:32

105. James 3:13-18

106. Michael Fletcher, *Empowering Leadership: How a Leadership Development Culture Builds Better Leaders Faster,* (Nashville, Tennessee: Thomas Nelson, 2018), 17-18

107. Genesis 2:2-3

108. Psalm 121:3-4

109. Proverbs 29:18

110. Curt Thompson, M.D., *The Soul of Shame: Retelling the Stories We Believe About Ourselves,* (Downers Grove, Illinois: InterVarsity Press, 2015) 29

111. Matthew 7:21-23

112. Romans 8:5

113. Ephesians 3:14-19

114. Nessa Carey, Ph.D., *The Epigenetics Revolution: How Modern Biology Is Rewriting Our Understanding of Genetics, Disease, and Inheritance,* (New York, New York: Columbia University Press, 2012), 235-236

115. Proverbs 4:23

116. Steven W. Porges, Ph.D., *The Pocket Guide to The Polyvagal Theory: The Transformative Power of Feeling Safe,* (New York – London: W.W. Norton & Company, 2017), 43, 51

117. Nessa Carey, Ph.D., *The Epigenetics Revolution: How Modern Biology Is Rewriting Our Understanding of Genetics, Disease, and Inheritance,* (New York, New York: Columbia University Press, 2012), 309

118. David Perlmutter, MD., *Brain Maker: The Power of Gut Microbes to Heal and Protect Your Brain-for Life,* (New York, New York: Little, Brown and Company, 2015), 25

119. 1 Corinthians 9:26-27

120. James 1:23-25

121. John 4:32122

122. Stephen W. Porges, Ph.D., The Pocket Guide to The Polyvagal Theory- The Transformative Power of Feeling Safe, (W.W. Norton & Company, Inc., New York, NY, 2017), 77

123. Rob Moll, *What Your Body Knows About God: How We Are Designed to Connect, Serve and Thrive,* (Downers Grove, Illinois: InterVarsity Press, 2014), 163. Andrew Newberg and Mark Robert Waldman, *How God Changes Your Brain: Breakthrough Findings from a Leading Neuroscientist,* (New York: Ballantine Books, 2010), 163

124. Ibid.,166

125. 1 Corinthians 3:2-3

126. Steven W. Porges, Ph.D., *The Pocket Guide to The Polyvagal Theory: The Transformative Power of Feeling Safe,* (New York – London: W.W. Norton & Company, 2017), 25-26

127. Jeremiah 17:9-19

128. Catherine Athans, Ph.D., *The Heart Brain: Did you know you have 3 Brains?,* (Los Altos, California: Angels Island Press, 2011), 6, 31

129. Matthew 18:3

130. 1 Corinthians 13:11

131. Matthew 6:15

132. Psalms 10:17

133. Psalm 100:4

134. Mark 2:27-28

135. Ephesians 4:11-13

136. Romans 10:4

137. 1 Timothy 1:17- 3:16

138. 1 Timothy 4:12-14

139. Henry Cloud, *Necessary Endings: The Employees, Businesses, and Relationships That All of Us Have to Give Up in Order to Move Forward*, (New York, New York: HarperCollins Publishers, 2010), 16

140. James 3:15

141. 1 Corinthians 1:18-2:16

142. Rick Warren, *The Purpose Driven Church*, (Grand Rapids, Michigan: Zondervan, 1995), 21

143. Luke 16:15

144. Joe Navarro, *What Every Body is Saying: An Ex-FBI Agent's Guide to Speed-Reading People,* (New York, New York: HarperCollins Publishers, 2008), 4

145. Ephesians :10

146. Philippians :12-13

17563629R00117

Made in the USA
Middletown, DE
04 December 2018